KUAN YIN

KUAN YIN

Myths and Revelations of the
Chinese Goddess of Compassion

Martin Palmer and Jay Ramsay
with Man-Ho Kwok

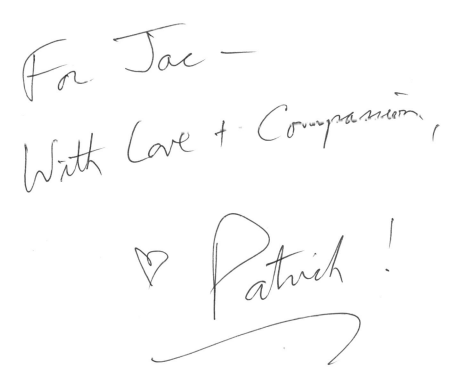

For Jac —
With Love + Compassion,

♡ Patrick !

Thorsons
An Imprint of HarperCollins*Publishers*
77–85 Fulham Palace Road
Hammersmith, London W6 8JB

1160 Battery Street
San Francisco, California 94111–1213

Published by Thorsons 1995

10 9 8 7 6 5 4 3

© ICOREC 1995

Illustrations © Circa Photo-library

Martin Palmer, Jay Ramsay and Man-Ho Kwok assert the moral right to
be identified as the authors of this work

A catalogue record for this book
is available from the British Library

ISBN 1 85538 417 5

Printed in Great Britain by Woolnough Bookbinding Ltd

for Lucy Lidell,
true healer, tantrika, teacher and friend

It is finished in beauty,
It is finished in beauty.

for Eli,
whose book this is.

Contents

Introduction xi

Part 1: The History and Origins of Kuan Yin 1

Part 2: The Myths and Legends of Kuan Yin 55

Part 3: The Poems of Kuan Yin 95

      Introduction by Martin Palmer 97

      Introduction by Jay Ramsay 106

      Using the Poems as Divination 113

      Kuan Yin the Quatrains: 1–100 119

Index 222

Index to poems 225

ACKNOWLEDGEMENTS

From Martin's side, special thanks to Shoji Hazama for hours of patient travel and answering questions; to colleagues in China, especially Peter Zhao; to my long-suffering colleagues in ICOREC and finally, reverence and love to the Goddess, even though she is not mine.

From Jay's side, special thanks to Carole for her guidance, Lucy as ever, Alan Rycroft, Gabriel Bradford Millar, Scarlett Laroma, Jonathan Mallard, Henry Shukman, Rae Beth – and the Goddess Herself.

Finally, warm thanks to Elizabeth Hutchins for her editorial expertise and Paula McCann for her sympathetic design.

INTRODUCTION

You can see her face almost anywhere in the world where the Chinese live. Visit any collection of Chinese paintings or statues in museums throughout the world and she is bound to be there. Visit any Chinese restaurant and most homes and her gentle face and elegant figure will welcome you. The Goddess of Compassion, Kuan Yin, is the most popular and widespread of any deity of Chinese religion. Yet she is barely known in the West and few studies of her have ever been made.

To the Chinese and many Koreans and Japanese, Kuan Yin, or Kannon, is the most important deity of all. Her influence extends from the very dawn of creation to the heartfelt wishes of women desiring children. In times of sickness and of trouble, she is the first to be invoked. She is child-bearer, creator, living compassion, friend and intercessor. She is the great goddess of life itself.

Kuan Yin knows no religious boundaries. She graces virtually all Taoist temples and all Sacred Mountains; she is found in almost all Chinese Buddhist temples; she is revered in Shintoism and even Christianity has an understanding of her and her significance.

To visit a Kuan Yin temple is to begin to understand her power. Take the temple dedicated to her in Macau, on the edge of southern China. This temple stretches back over 600 years and is one of the largest temples in Macau. As you enter, you are greeted by the figure of Sakyamuni Buddha – the historical Buddha. To most in the West, he is seen as the centre point of Buddhism. But here, Prince Gautama Siddhartha, the Buddha, is just a door-keeper, guarding the far more important deity beyond, the goddess Kuan Yin. Only after you have passed by and paid obeisance to the Buddhas of the Past, the Present and the Future are you at last admitted into the heart of the temple, the shrine room of the goddess herself.

Kuan Shih Yin, to accord her her full title, is the One who Hears the Cries of the World. She is the living expression of loving compassion; the one who will come to your aid; the one who offers a caring aspect to the otherwise somewhat remote world-view of much of Chinese Buddhism with its scales of merit and demerit, its hells and rebirths, its retributions and consequences in this life and beyond. Kuan Yin will break the cycle of rebirth, of punishment and of retribution for you. She will save you from perils of this world and the next – and the next! If you are desperate for a child, you turn to her, for she brings children. If you are sick, you turn to her for healing. If you are in danger, you pray to her for deliverance. She is all pervasive, all loving, the very embodiment of beauty and grace. It is hardly surprising that she is so popular.

Perhaps because she is religiously promiscuous, having started life as a male Buddhist Bodhisattva, Kuan Yin has become the great female deity and goddess, revered across faiths. Perhaps it is because no school of meditation or philosophy has ever arisen around her; her following is amongst ordinary people who know the need for compassion. Perhaps it is just good old sexism, for she is almost alone in the pantheon of Chinese Buddhism as a woman, and, while Taoism has goddesses, she is of a different kind, much more powerful and universally adored. She is the feminine in Chinese religion. Not everyone is comfortable with that, however. She has been ignored by most scholars and few in the West know the great legends about her or understand her place in the hearts of the Chinese.

But why should she be of any interest to the West? Precisely because she does embody the feminine in Chinese religion and opens the door to an exploration of other divine feminine images in this ancient culture. But also, perhaps more importantly, because she offers a vision of the divine feminine which transcends one particular religion, drawing upon diverse sources and being adored by followers of a number of faiths. In a world which is increasingly recognizing the importance of pluralism, the celebration of diversity and the reality of accepting difference, she stands as almost a patron saint or patron goddess of such a realization. Added to this is the recognition of the need to rediscover and re-articulate the feminine in the divine, which is so profoundly affecting the patriarchies of Judaism and Christianity. In such a swirl of changes and refocusing, Kuan Yin offers a model of how this has all happened before.

In the religiously pluralist divine feminine of Kuan Yin, graceful Goddess of Compassion, we can glimpse what for many in the West has been a missing dimension of our spirituality. In her salvationary mode she reminds us of our need for help in a world which often seems to say, 'Stand on your own feet or sink.' In her limitless compassion she offers hope of change and transformation, not wrought just by miracles but by redeeming and transforming what is inherent within each of us.

So who or what is Kuan Yin?

The search for her origins and her significance will take us back into history and deep into the need for the feminine in religion. It involves exploring myths and legends and travelling from the furthest western borders of China to the islands at the easternmost point of the country. Kuan Yin is a dangerous goddess, because she is not easily confined by doctrines, creeds or dogmas. Over the centuries, there have been many different attempts to explain her or to define her.

Our quest for Kuan Yin starts with the coming of Buddhism in a popular form to China, where it flows into the quest for the divine feminine of ancient China. From there we turn to look at the transformation of a male Bodhisattva into a female goddess of mercy whose physical model comes from the ancient faith of Egypt via Christianity and the Virgin Mary.

Flowing out of northwest China, the story takes us across China in search of miraculous tales and legends, mountain-top monasteries and strange monks and scriptures. The journey takes in the cultural city of Hangchow and then washes onto the beach of Pu To island, the most sacred site in the worship of Kuan Yin and one of the four Sacred Mountains of Chinese Buddhism.

The stories of Kuan Yin are amongst some of the best and most exciting of ancient China. These are explored in Part Two before we move to the *100 Prophecies of Kuan Yin*. This extraordinary collection of poems is used daily as a source of divination and also contains some of the loveliest poems of Imperial China. Through Jay's rendering of our English translation of these great poems, the door is opened to hear the quiet voice of Kuan Yin offering guidance, wisdom and, above all, compassion to the world today.

Perhaps the neglect of Kuan Yin by Western scholars of China is now coming to an end because what she represents is beginning to make sense to a world seeking to recover the divine feminine and the nature of divinity in diversity.

We invite you to travel with us on a unique journey which is the story of Kuan Yin, the Compassionate Companion.

1

THE HISTORY AND ORIGINS OF KUAN YIN

The History and Origins of Kuan Yin

The Compassionate Bodhisattva

At some time around the first century AD, a remarkable Buddhist text was composed in Sanskrit, somewhere in the northern parts of India or possibly in areas of what is now Afghanistan. It is known in Sanskrit as the *Saddharma Pundarika Sutra* – the Sutra of the Lotus of the Wondrous Law. More commonly it is simply known as the Lotus Sutra. It is a key text of the Mahayana Buddhist tradition.

There are two main forms of Buddhism. The Theravada tradition – meaning the Teachings of the Elders – sticks to a strict understanding of the teachings of the historical Buddha. It teaches personal individual struggle to find the Path to enlightenment. This is hard, not often achieved and takes years, sometimes many lives, to achieve.

The second form of Buddhism is called Mahayana, the Great Vehicle tradition. This tradition feels that the individualism and difficulty of the Theravada tradition is unnecessary. It presents a vision of the Buddha and of Buddhism which is accessible to all, religious and lay person alike. It offers the possibility of release from the cycle of suffering and death and rebirth. This comes through personal devotion and reliance upon the salvationary activities of various intermediaries known as Bodhisattvas. Through countless lives of perfection Bodhisattvas have acquired great merit which they use to free those who suffer. Mahayana Buddhism is called the Great Vehicle because its teachings are like a vast wagon capable of carrying many to release from rebirth.

It is from this Great Vehicle tradition that the Lotus Sutra comes. This sutra claims to have been given by the historical Buddha but depicts a mythological world and time. The text opens thus:

> Once the Buddha was staying at the City of Royal Palaces and on the Vulture Peak assembled a great host of his greater monks, in all twelve thousand.
>
> The Buddha sent forth from the curl of white hair between his eyebrows a ray of light, which illuminated eighteen thousand worlds in the eastern quarter, so that there was nowhere it did not reach, downwards to the lowest hell and upward to the highest Heaven of each world.[1]

This is clearly a dramatic text and it is considered one of the greatest Buddhist texts in the world. Its vision of a compassionate Buddha who sends forth the light of enlightenment and salvation to the whole world has made it a cornerstone of the Mahayana tradition of Buddhism.

We know nothing of the writer. But he or she was inspired, for the Lotus Sutra is one of the most beautiful and graceful texts in the religious world. Its place in the affections of the people of China and Japan is unrivalled.

To give you a sense of the salvationary and compassionate nature of this text, let me quote from Chapter 25, a chapter of immense importance with regard to Kuan Yin and her evolution. It tells of a Bodhisattva called Avalokitesvara. The name means 'The Lord who Regards the Cries of the World'. This Bodhisattva had lived lives of such exemplary quality as to have eliminated all his own karma, which creates rebirth, and to have built up a store of merit with which he wished to help free all life from the struggle of life and death. Thus delaying his final release into the nothingness of Nirvana, he hears the cries of the world and pours out his compassion on those who seek release from the wheel of suffering.

In the earliest part of the chapter, the Buddha describes the effects of calling upon the compassion of Avalokitesvara:

> If any, carried away by a flood, call upon his name, they will immediately reach the shallows . . . Or if anyone cries who is

in deadly peril by the sword, the sword will be snapped asunder. If wicked demons attack, the one who cries will become invisible to them . . . If a woman desires a son, worships and pays homage, she will bear a son, virtuous and wise; or if a daughter, then of good demeanour and looks.

The text goes on to say that this Bodhisattva can take on any form in order to reach a person in need of salvation. He can appear as one of the Hindu gods such as Brahma or Indra to help Hindus; as a monk or nun, as male or female, depending upon the needs of the time, the person and the place. The text continues by reflecting upon the nature of this compassion:

> Every evil state of existence,
> hells and ghosts and animals,
> Sorrows of birth, age, disease, death,
> All will thus be ended for him.
> True Regard, serene Regard,
> Far-reaching, wise Regard,
> Regard of pity, Regard compassionate,
> Ever longed for, ever looked for
> In radiance ever pure and serene!
> Wisdom's sun, destroying darkness,
> Subduer of woes, of storm, of fire,
> Illuminator of the world!
> Law of pity, thunder quivering,
> Compassion wondrous as a great cloud,
> Pouring spiritual rain like nectar,
> Quenching all the flames of distress!

Little wonder that such a magnificent vision should inspire those across the vast lands of China who long for release.

But what does this have to do with Kuan Yin? It is that when rendered into Chinese, the Sanskrit title Avalokitesvara becomes Kuan Shih Yin – 'The One who Hears the Cries of the World'. Kuan Yin begins life as the Chinese Avalokitesvara.

The Lotus Sutra was one of the earliest Buddhist texts to be translated into Chinese. The greatest of these translations was by a master translator, Kumarajiva.

From the evidence of his name, Kumarajiva was not Chinese. It is said that he was a prisoner sold into slavery and that he originally came either from Taxila, in what is now northern Pakistan, close to Afghanistan, or from Kharashar in Turkestan. His skills as a translator were soon recognized and from AD 397 to 415 he lived in Chang-an, the capital city of the state of Ch'in in China. He completed his translation of the Lotus Sutra into Chinese in AD 406, giving it the title *Miao Fa Lien Hua Ching*. This translation was neither the first nor the last into Chinese, but it is considered the most sublime and is the one most favoured in China to this day.

Thus the name Kuan Shih Yin entered the Chinese world and the story begin to unfold.

The Shift to the Female

The compassionate nature of Kuan Shih Yin obviously appealed to many for whom the more austere teachings of the

Buddha had little appeal. From the fifth century AD onwards statues of the Bodhisattva began to appear in China. At this stage, Kuan Shih Yin was always depicted as a man, albeit one very slight and graceful of form and visage. For example, the British Museum has in its Chinese collection a very fine life-size statue of Kuan Shih Yin which dates from the Six Dynasties – AD 550 to 577. This statue is clearly male, though somewhat androgynous, as are many of the male forms of Kuan Yin.

By the late eighth century AD, however, Kuan Yin began to be regularly depicted as female. What happened and why?

It is a difficult detective job to try and discern the time and place where the shift from male Avalokitesvara to female Kuan Yin took place. In Kumarajiva's translation, and indeed in all the earliest translations of the Lotus Sutra, Kuan Shih Yin

is indisputably male. While it is recognized within the text that he is capable of taking a female form, this is not considered his main form. The Buddhist pilgrim Hsuan Tsang (c.596–664), in his prodigious records of his travels from China to India, makes no mention of a female Kuan Yin, only male. In texts such as the *Cheng Ming Ching*, which dates from the end of the seventh century, Kuan Yin is still male and clearly so. Kuan Yin is also clearly male in the Surangama Sutra, which was first produced in AD 705 in Chinese. Claiming to be a translation from an original Sanskrit text, it now seems certain that this text was written in Chinese in China at about that time. It indicates a growing interest in Kuan Yin, but again, not in a female form.

It is possible to chart the rise in devotion to Kuan Yin through the statues and dedications inscribed in the great Buddhist caves of Lung Men, near Loyang, Henan province. Those made from AD 500 to 540 show that the historical Buddha, Sakyamuni, was the most popular Buddhist figure. There were 43 dedications to him, with 35 to the future Buddha, Maitraya, 8 to Amida, the Buddha of the Western Paradise, another salvationary figure in Buddhism, and 22 to Kuan Yin.

From 650 to 690, the dedications show a radical shift. Only 8 are to Sakyamuni, 11 to Maitraya; 103 to Amida and 44 to Kuan Yin. The desire for a salvationary, compassionate face to Buddhism could not be more clearly signalled than in the rise to popularity of both Kuan Yin and Amida, a trend which has never been reversed.[2]

By the mid to late ninth century, as dedications from the Buddhist manuscripts found in the sealed caves of Tun Huang confirm, worship of Kuan Yin had not only become a major cult but Kuan Yin was now usually considered and depicted as female. This is borne out by the sculpture and painting which have survived from that time.

So something happened between the early eighth century and the mid ninth century to turn Kuan Yin from a male into a female figure. What could it be?

It is impossible to know exactly, but there are some fascinating clues, psychological, archaeological and philosophical. Though occasionally difficult to discern through the passage of time, these nevertheless give a hint as to what happened.

The cult of Kuan Yin grew most strongly and rapidly from the seventh to the ninth centuries AD in a wild part of China where numerous cultures met and interacted. Kuan Yin's roots lie not in the heartlands of historic China, but on the northwest frontier, on the Silk Road. It is here that some of the earliest images of the goddess have been found and it is here that the texts found in the Tun Huang caves were written, texts with paeans of praise to Kuan Yin. The caves were sealed with literally tens of thousands of texts hidden in them sometime around the end of the tenth or beginning of the eleventh century AD.

It was from China's wild northwest border that her cult spread across China and on to Japan. The male cult of Kuan Yin had already penetrated as a result of the dissemination of the Lotus Sutra, but the distinctive female forms of Kuan Yin only began to fan out extensively from the north west in the ninth to tenth centuries.

THE NEED FOR THE DIVINE FEMININE

The need for a female aspect of the divine runs deep within many, if not all cultures. The earliest pantheons of China are a mixture of male and female and half-human, half-animal beings. For example, the two great founder-figures of Chinese culture, agriculture, religion and language are Fu Hsi and Nua Kua. These magical, mythical figures are the progenitors of 'Chinese-ness'. Fu Hsi is male and Nua Kua is female and both of them are half-human and half-snake. Together they created all the aspects of civilization – writing, agriculture, medicine, astrology – and gave them as gifts to humanity. Together they ruled as man and woman, guiding the child-like earliest peoples. They are considered the first two of the Three August Ones of Chinese pre-history, of Chinese mythology.

Chinese mythology in its earliest forms appears to have been neither patriarchal nor matriarchal, but was what Riane Eisler has called *gylanic*[3] – a world where male and female were equal. Other legends of China reinforce this, as does climbing the oldest and most sacred of the Taoist Sacred Mountains of China, T'ai Shan. All the way up the sacred path leading to the summit of this extraordinary mountain are shrines and statues of the great goddess of the mountain. She has many titles: Old Mother, Old Grandmother of T'ai, the Heavenly Immortal deity Green Jade Mother and the Goddess of the Azure Clouds. Amongst the host of legends about her, one recounts that she and her brother, the Jade Emperor, the rulers of Heaven, descended to Earth on T'ai Shan. Here they brought to life all the creatures and plants, birds and fishes. From this mountain streamed forth life in its multitudinous forms. Last of all, the goddess made human beings. *Made* them, not gave birth to them, for there seems to be no tradition in China of an earth mother figure. As brother and sister the god and goddess ruled the world from the mountain before ascending again.

Today, almost all trace of this legend has gone, overlaid with much more conventionally acceptable patriarchal concepts. Now the Jade Emperor has the highest point of the mountain as his sole preserve. Yet the tradition is not all gone. For to enter onto the plateau of the summit itself, you must pass through the Gate to Heaven. This literally is a gate, set into the chasm which leads to the plateau. Behind it is a courtyard where three deities sit and before whom you must pass to enter. The one opposite the gate is the god of T'ai Shan himself. But on either side are Kuan Yin and the goddess of T'ai Shan, the Old Mother, the creator of human beings. There is no entry to the plateau without devotion to all three. As will be seen later, the link to Kuan Yin here is no accident.

In other legends, the goddess of T'ai Shan is called the Daughter of Heaven and is again credited with the creation of human beings. This is why the Emperors of China so often came to worship at T'ai Shan, the first recorded visit being that of the great tyrant and unifier of China, Chin Shi Huang Ti, who visited around 218 BC. The rulers came because, being the Sons of Heaven, they had to make obeisance to their Heavenly Mother.

The role of women in the sphere of the divine in ancient China, before Confucian values came to influence Chinese society from the fourth century BC onwards, seems to bear out Eisler's vision of the existence of a culture in which men and women were equal. There is no evidence that I have seen to show that any form of matriarchal society existed in China in any major way. Rather, it was a society of equals. This seems to be borne out by the fact that both men and women were considered capable of being shamans – vehicles for communication between the spirit world and the material world.

Shamanism can lay claim to being the oldest world religion. Originating at least 8,000 years ago in Siberia, it spread across the then existing land bridge between Siberia and Alaska, and thus down through North America. It is the basis for much of what we now know as Native American religion. In similar fashion, it spread down into China and Korea and across to Japan. Its traces here are to be found in much of contemporary Taoism and in aspects of Shinto in Japan. Its influence spread west along the migration routes of the steppe peoples, reaching into northern Europe, where traces of it are to be found in Finland and Norway, and south beyond China into South East Asia.

The heart of shamanism is a belief in two worlds: the material, physical world which we inhabit and experience, and the superior, spiritual world, which exists alongside this world and sometimes breaks through into it. The role and power of the shaman is his or her ability to communicate between these worlds. This is done through trance states and through being taken over by an animal spirit – in Siberia and much of northern China, usually the spirit of a bear.

Through such states, the shaman could ask questions of the spirit world concerning problems in the material world such as illness or disaster. The concern of shamanism is to help humanity live in accordance with the wishes and flow of the spiritual world. To be out of kilter with the spiritual world is to be in trouble. To be in the flow of the spiritual world is to go with the forces of life. This notion lies behind the later developments of Taoism, especially as expressed in the *Tao Te Ching*, where the goal of human existence is to be part of the Tao, the Way, that flows on and on forever.

There is, as yet, little evidence of a major mother goddess culture in China. But it is important to stress that there is also no evidence of any serious patriarchal society there until about the time of the Shang dynasty (*c.*1700–1100 BC). Yet it is also at this time that we first find written evidence of strange figures who seem to come from the earliest period of Chinese religion – the Eastern and Western Mothers. An oracle bone text from the

Shang dynasty talks about making offerings to these two goddesses. We know nothing about these two figures, though their association with cosmic directions is perhaps significant, as that would appear to indicate that they were celestial mothers in the same way that Nua Kua and the goddess of T'ai Shan are celestial rather than earth mother figures.

The next significant reference to a mother goddess comes in the *I Ching*, written somewhere around the eleventh to tenth century BC. Hexagram 35 line two says:

> To prosper is also to grieve. The oracle says good fortune.
> He will receive great protection and blessing from the
> ancestral Queen Mother.[4]

It is unusual for any deity or divinity to be named in the text of the *I Ching* and so this inclusion is quite significant. The term 'ancestral Queen Mother' denotes that she is the mother deity of the Chou tribes, tribes which emerged from the wilderness to the west of China and whose temple was on the Chou Sacred Mountain of Ch'i Shan – in the west. Perhaps it was this ancestral mother who gave rise to the title 'Queen Mother of the West'?

The *Tao Te Ching*, written *c.* fourth century BC, speaks of the feminine aspect in the coming to life of the universe. Dealing more with philosophical concepts than with folk wisdom or legend, it nevertheless echoes the notion of the life-bringing Heavenly Mother which has been so clearly discerned in the earlier texts. For example Chapter 1 says:

> Nothing – the nameless
>   is the beginning;
> While Heaven, the mother
>   is the creatrix of all things.
>
> All mysteries are Tao, and Heaven is their mother:
> She is the gateway and the womb-door.[5]

Chapter 52 is even more explicit:

> Every living thing
> Comes from the Mother of Us All:

If we can understand the Mother
Then we can understand her children;

And if we know ourselves as children
We can see the source as Her.[6]

What is even more significant about these odd references is that the feminine, the mother, is not identified with the Earth. Quite the reverse in fact. She is a Heavenly figure, a protogenitrix who is not the passive, receptive earth mother penetrated by some sky father, as in so many ancient cultures. Instead she is of Heaven itself. The cosmos is her womb. This is to be discerned in some of the classic imagery of Chinese poetry and prose. For example, the phrase, 'Heaven broke open, the Earth surged forth', which is the exact translation of the first line of the first of the *100 Prophecies of Kuan Yin* and an image found in regular use in Chinese poetry, seems to indicate an eruption of both Heaven and Earth from some primal containment – the womb perhaps of all life, as the *Tao Te Ching* says.

This lack of an earth goddess figure seems linked to the lack of any matriarchal religion in pre-historic China. I realize that this goes against much of the conventional thinking of the mother goddess literature which is emerging, but it is perhaps not without significance that none of these studies (such as Marija Gimbutas's major studies of the mother goddess) looks at China. China would seem to present us with a very different model from that posited by many scholars or explorers of the divine feminine. It posits a world in which male and female deities as well as male and female shamans/religious figures worked together. This continued in some form or another at least until the fifth century BC when the firm hand of Confucian patriarchy began to exclude the feminine and the shamanistic – indeed the whole emotional world was sacrificed to the demands of law, order, filial piety and control. The extraordinary collection of shamanistic poems and songs called *Chu Tzu*, the 'Songs of the South', written down in the fourth to first centuries BC, reflect this earlier world, but they are the last major expression of shamanism until its re-emergence in the Taoism of popular belief of the second century AD. This is something I explore further on.

In the Warring States period (403–221 BC), and more particularly in the Han dynasty (206 BC–AD 220), accounts of a Queen Mother of Heaven begin to appear, in reaction, I would maintain, to the suppression of the older shamanistic models. For as the old ways were discredited, it began to be necessary for the goddess to appear more united, more central and thus more powerful to withstand the dismissive attitudes of the Confucians. As Suzanne Cahill says:

> Various texts seem to describe several different goddesses, each called Hsi Wang Mu – Queen Mother of the West. Perhaps these deities represent different local cults and social strata. They include a teacher, a directional deity, spirits of the holy mountains, a divine weaver, a shaman and a star goddess.[7]

In this period, the figure of the Queen Mother of the West draws to it the variety of strands outlined by Cahill above. And what emerges is a strong, tough and distant goddess, involved with creation and in advising the earliest rulers, but distant from ordinary affairs.

She is set in the west, which for the Chinese is the direction of paradise, of the true mystics and of mystery itself. It is from the west that the divine breaks through into China. It was from the western mountain – Ch'i Shan – that the oracles of the *I Ching* were given, including the one quoted above about the ancestral Queen Mother. It is to the west that Lao Tzu goes for enlightenment. At the gateway to the west, so legend says, he wrote the *Tao Te Ching*. And it was a dream about the west which traditionally laid the seeds for the coming of Buddhism to China.

One night, the Emperor Ming (AD 58–75) had a dream. In it he saw a golden deity flying before his palace. Upon awakening, the Emperor asked his advisers what this could mean. One of them, Fu Yi, said he had heard that in the west there had been a sage who had achieved release and who was called the Buddha. He was able to fly and was of a golden colour. The Emperor was greatly pleased and sent an envoy to the west to obtain a statue of this Buddha and his teachings.

This story is almost certainly a legend rather than historically accurate, but it does show the role of the mystic west in China. In trying to understand why a cult which developed in the northwest of China should spread and be accepted, it is worth holding in mind that the west was the direction of divine intervention in China – in much the same way as the east has been in Western thought.

In taking you through this exploration of the goddess figures and the role of the west, I have tried to indicate that Kuan Yin did not appear from nowhere. There were elements in Chinese belief and culture which could contribute towards the development of a major goddess cult. But this does not explain why, at some time in the eighth or ninth century, the Chinese took the unprecedented step of creating a new, female deity by transforming an existing male one. To understand this we need to go a little deeper.

Let us return to the figure of the Queen Mother of the West. As indicated above, she probably emerged from the general shamanistic background of China. She is certainly strongly associated with shamanism. For example, *The Songs of the South*, containing material from the fourth century BC to the first century AD, have many references to goddesses and to the Queen Mother of the West. In many cases, though not always, the goddesses are depicted as fierce and distant. As for the Queen Mother, she emerges from these shamanistic texts as the sort of remote deity with whom the shamans would communicate. Her interest in this world is limited and only evoked by the supplications and entreaties that reach her through the shaman. In *The Classic of the Mountains and the Seas*, a strange book of fact and fiction dating from around the fourth century BC, she is clearly depicted as a shamanistic deity:

> Another 350 *li* to the west is a mountain called Jade Mountain. This is the place where the Queen Mother of the West dwells. As for the Queen Mother of the West, her appearance is like that of a human, with a leopard's tail and tiger's teeth. Moreover she is skilled at whistling. In her disheveled hair she wears a *sheng* headdress. She is controller of the Grindstone and the Five Shards Constellations of the Heavens.[8]

By the end of the Han period (third century AD), however, she had undergone quite a transformation. This was at least in part because shamanism had been very successfully attacked, ridiculed and ostracized by the court Confucians. It was now considered primitive and uncultured.

The shamans had exercised immense influence in the early courts of China. They dominated the Shang dynasty and were very powerful still under the Chou (*c.*1050–770 BC). But gradually they lost their grip on power and when the Confucians began to emerge as a serious administrative group, they saw the shamans as their natural enemies. Where Confucianism sought logic and control, shamans spoke for and of a world of spirits and uncontrollable forces. Over the period from around the fourth century BC to the second century AD, the Confucians waged a long and slow struggle against the influence of the shamans at court and in the social affairs of the country. They were largely successful, forcing shamanism to go underground from whence it re-emerged in certain forms of popular Taoism from the second century AD onwards. But what is significant for us in this struggle is that any deity which was locked into the earlier shamanistic world-view either had to undergo a thorough redefinition in Confucian terms or he or she was out in the cold. The Queen Mother of the West partially underwent such a rehabilitation. But she was so deeply associated with the earlier world-view that she was never fully accepted into the newly emerging Confucian one.

This is perhaps rather tragically highlighted in the cult of the Queen Mother of the West which broke out in northeast China around 10 BC to AD 5. This cult was found amongst the poor rural peasantry. Through its apocalyptic dimensions – the people expected the coming of the Queen Mother and the heralding of a happier time – it aroused the peasantry to clamour for better living conditions. Inspired by the hope of a better future and feeling they had a powerful deity on their side, the peasants revolted. This unrest was eventually put down, but the un-Confucian aspects of this dangerous goddess were duly noted, even if later Confucian scholars would interpret these disturbances as forewarnings sent by Heaven of the collapse of the Former Han (206 BC–AD 8).

Popular Taoism arose from the second to third centuries AD. For the first time in Chinese religious history, it posited the possibility of personal salvation. In the earliest religious systems of China, the individual's spiritual well-being had been irrelevant. The role of the shaman or the religious role of the ruler had been to ensure that the world in general and the kingdom in particular was stable and good. But gradually the desire for personal or individual salvation began to appear. It first manifested itself in any significant way with the Five Bushels sect founded by the Taoist popularist Chang Tao Ling in the second century AD. This sect offered release from the consequences of past actions through rituals of redemption and salvation. It was so called after the amount of rice needed to buy redemption. Offering a personal sense of purpose and a place within the divine ordering of the world, it was immensely popular. Sects such as the Five Bushels sect increased in number and spread across vast areas of China.

The Rivalry of Taoism and Buddhism

With the coming of Mahayana Buddhism as a significant religious force from the fourth to fifth centuries AD onwards, the pursuit of personal release or salvation was fed by another stream, and there was a major struggle for the souls and minds of the ordinary Chinese. I have already pointed out how popular the Lotus Sutra was because it revealed a broad path to salvation or release, open to just about everyone. But at first, this attractive dimension of Buddhism was not apparent. Much of the Buddhism which first crossed over the mountains from India and from the areas of present day Afghanistan was obscure and hard to apply to everyday life. It was only when such doctrines as the compassionate outpourings of the Bodhisattvas began to be translated into Chinese that Buddhism really began to get a hold on the popular imagination.

Yet there was a great problem. Buddhism is a male-dominated faith. At this time it lacked a divine feminine aspect. In the wider world of Chinese belief, devotion to the Queen Mother of the West and other powerful creator or local female deities had been taken over by the resurgent forms of shamanism, namely popular Taoism and especially the Mao Shan sect of Taoism, whose central scriptures were, interestingly enough, revealed to them by the spirit of a woman shaman who it was believed had become an immortal. The Queen Mother of the West was drawn into the scriptures thus revealed, the Shang Ch'ing texts, and in them became one of the most powerful deities.

The Confucians may have won the battle for male supremacy at court, in official life and in scholarship, but outside, in the lives of the ordinary people, the divine feminine was alive and well, and now officially structured into Taoism, which was about to face its greatest challenge prior to the assaults of Communism this century.

Mao Shan Taoism became the most successful and powerful of the new Taoist schools throughout the period of the T'ang and Sung dynasties (AD 618–907, 960–1280), even being officially adopted by some of the T'ang Emperors. By the time of the T'ang dynasty there was a distinct rivalry between Taoism and Buddhism at both court and popular level. This is very significant for the rise of Kuan Yin, as we shall see.

Essentially, Taoism resented the inroads being made by this foreign religion, while Buddhism dismissed and ridiculed the shamanistic and folk religion elements of Taoism. This reached its peak in Taoist books such as the *Hua Hu Ching*, Record of Lao Tzu's Discourses with Foreigners, written *c.* seventh century AD, which claimed that when Lao Tzu, the mysterious founder figure of Taoism, went west, he went to India and founded a philosophy school. Here he taught a young and rather arrogant prince who took himself off before he had really grasped much of what Lao Tzu was talking about. The young prince, according to the Taoists, was none other than Prince Siddhartha Gautama, the Buddha! This, they said, explains why Buddhism is such a poorly thought through religion – just a pale imitation of Taoism!

The struggle reached a particularly unpleasant low point in AD 845 when the Taoists gained sufficient control of the court to order the destruction of all Buddhist temples and the return of all monks and nuns to lay life. According to records, 4,600 monasteries and 40,000 temples were destroyed and 260,000 monks and nuns and 150,000 of their slaves were returned to lay life.

The Buddhists replied during this period in like fashion, casting aspersions upon Taoist priests and monks and mocking the rituals of Taoist groups. It was a period of intense rivalry.

But the Taoists had a goddess.

Buddhism is very similar to Christianity in that it is a patriarchal, male dominated faith. Its central figure is the male Buddha who gives up wife and child to achieve his own enlightenment. The Buddhist pantheon was originally exclusively male. This reflects the cultures from which Buddhism emerged, where the role of the woman was a lowly one. The Buddha himself did not believe that women were sufficiently high on the scale of evolutionary rebirth to be capable of being religious – that is to say, nuns. It took a lot of persuasion by his faithful follower Ananda to make him change his mind. Buddhism is essentially patriarchal.

But the feminine aspect of the divine is something which given half a chance (which it isn't always afforded) will emerge. In Christianity, the Virgin Mary, the Mother of God, fulfils that purpose. It is clear that the longing for a female deity is strong within most cultures. The rise of the Virgin Mary in Christianity, of Sophia – Wisdom – in the Judaism of the Diaspora, of the various Taras in Tibetan Buddhism and the role of the goddesses in Hinduism all indicate in differing ways that the divine feminine is an essential part of religious life for many cultures.

Many feminist scholars are now claiming that before the rise of the major patriarchal religions such as Judaism, Buddhism, Christianity and Islam, worship of the divine feminine was widespread and dominant. Indeed, most posit the existence of a matriarchal religion which was deliberately suppressed by the rise of patriarchy. China does not support this view. Instead what appears to have existed in the earliest times was a society, as I have said before, where men and women were equals, as reflected in the Heavenly brother and sister stories. It was not matriarchy which patriarchy suppressed in China, but shamanism. The attack of the court, of the Confucians and of the rationalists in China from the sixth century BC onwards was on shamanism, complete with gods, goddesses, male and female shamans and the whole culture of oracles and divination.

Confucianism, too, is avowedly patriarchal. The teaching of a hierarchy of life with the male Emperor at the top, the father above the son and the son above the daughter constantly places women in the lowest rung of each section of the hierarchy. This was further intensified by the insistence that only male offspring were of any real significance. Hence the great importance of child-bringer goddesses. But despite the official line, the divine feminine was never crushed out of China's soul. Instead it has survived by adapting, as in the case of the Queen Mother of the West or Kuan Yin, or by persisting in certain areas through the sheer popularity of a specific cult.

Of all the shrines on T'ai Shan, the greatest of the Taoist Sacred Mountains, the one which I found most moving was a small cave shrine, about three-quarters of a mile from the summit. Here, in a cavern thick with centuries of incense, sits a squat, crude statue of the Old Grandmother of the Mountain. The cave is tiny and within a great boulder-like protuberance on the side of the path. Banners hung outside proclaim the deity within and, during the daytime, only women appeared to be making offerings. But as we descended by moonlight, we found that of all the shrines and temples on the route, this one was the busiest and that it was now the turn of the men, the coolies who labour up and down the mountain for a living, to come and worship. The cave has about it an aura unlike anything else on the mountain and speaks more powerfully than anything else there of the pre-Taoist, shamanistic faith which first elevated this great mountain to a divine status. Such stories can be repeated all over China, at those places where the numinous seems most powerfully to break through into the physical world.

The divine feminine in China appears to function at two distinct levels. At an official level of mythology and teaching, all the divine women, including the Queen Mother of the West or Kuan Yin, are nominally under the authority of male deities – the Buddha or the Jade Emperor, for example. The fear of the power of the feminine in Buddhism, where Kuan Yin's sexuality causes the official teachers to claim her female form is just for this world, has been noted earlier. In Taoism, there is no fear of the divine feminine as such, though in mainstream Taoist thought, especially the monastic versions, women are viewed as deadly traps. Their role in the sexual manuals of Taoism is only as an aid to the spiritual development of the male master.

But at a popular level, the divine feminine works in quite a different way. For the ordinary people, faced with a world of Taoist and Buddhist hells, demons, angry gods and stern Buddhas, it is the compassionate, caring, loving and nurturing aspects of the divine which they flock to, be that the salvationary Amida Buddha, ruler of the Paradise of the West, who will rescue the downtrodden and the pious, or Kuan Yin, who will rescue and tend those in trouble. At a popular level, the divine feminine is probably the most important aspect of the pantheon of deities, and while a nod might be given to standard theology in which the male deities, Buddhas, etc., are supposed to be most important, it is ignored in practice, by both men and women. What Chinese religion shows is that the divine feminine has always had a central role, even if religious orthodoxy finds that impossible to admit – a not dissimilar case to Christianity and the role of the Mother of God/Virgin Mary.

Returning to the past, as the demand for and response to salvationary religion, both Buddhist and Taoist, grew and grew in China throughout the major part of the first millennium AD, the role of the divine feminine became more and more important.

By the eighth century AD, Taoism had a series of well developed female deities of considerable power and authority – the Queen Mother of the West being one of the most powerful and widespread. Buddhism at this point had no female deity. Instead it offered some rather stern male Buddhas and Bodhisattvas, relieved only by such compassionate figures as the male Kuan Yin and the male Amida Buddha, who rescues people from suffering and brings them to bliss in his Paradise in the West, Sukhavati.

What Buddhism needed was a female form of the divine to reach out to the ordinary people, to compete with the Taoist's Queen Mother of the West and other local female deities such as the various sea goddesses, and to offer salvation to the masses.

I am not saying that the Chinese Buddhists sat down and planned Kuan Yin the goddess. Changes and developments in religious thought rarely happen that way! But the forces which were being brought to bear upon Buddhism by the competition with Taoism and in the general groundswell of popular religion fused around the eighth century to produce a new deity – or rather to reshape and refocus an older one, the male Kuan Yin.

Yet the deep-seated sexism of all patriarchal religions is hard to dislodge. Thus it is that many studies of Kuan Yin in Chinese will stress that she is only in female form because this world is so corrupt and degenerate that this is the only way Kuan Yin can be understood. These writers claim that once she does leave the world of suffering and struggle and enters Nirvana, she will revert to her male form: 'After considering all divergent views and historical facts, it would perhaps be safe to say that Kuan Yin was a female while on earth but turned a male after ascending to Heaven.'[9]

As already mentioned, the emergence of a feminine Kuan Yin took place in northwest China, fulfilling again the notion that truth and revelation come to China from the west. What is perhaps most extraordinary about this new deity is that one element which almost certainly contributed to the creation of Kuan Yin came from very far west.

THE COMING OF CHRISTIANITY

In AD 635, Christianity in its Nestorian form officially entered the Chinese capital of Chang-an. In that year, Bishop Alopen from Persia was welcomed into the city by the Emperor and given all the facilities and help needed to establish the Church in the capital and across China.

The branch of Christianity which had made its way to China was a form considered heretical by the West. It is called Nestorian after a deposed former Archbishop of Constantinople who died around AD 450 and who had declared that Mary was not the Mother of God because that smacked of mother goddess worship. He insisted that she be simply known as 'the Mother of Christ'. For fascinating reasons which I have explored elsewhere,[10] Nestorius was deposed and his views declared heretical.

At this time, the Church in Persia was constantly under threat because it was seen as the faith of the Persian Empire's greatest rival, Rome. For complex reasons, the Persian Christians adopted a form of Nestorius's teachings and thus came to be seen as being themselves opposed to the orthodoxy of the Roman or Byzantine Empire. With the west blocked to them for religious and political reasons, the Nestorian Christians of Persia spread south into Arabia (one of them was the monk who first introduced Muhammad to monotheism), into India and into Central Asia and China.

In Central Asia, along the trade routes such as the Silk Road, they were very influential, being primarily traders. It is certain that Christianity was being practised in towns along the edges of the Silk Road by the sixth century. Indeed, Nestorian Christianity enjoyed considerable favour with the Turkish and Mongolian tribes in that area from the seventh century onwards, competing

for a while with Tibetan Buddhism for the souls of the
Mongolians and northern Tibetans.

OUT OF THE MELTING-POT

In the area of northwest China during the centuries of the T'ang
dynasty (AD 618–907) a host of different faiths rubbed shoulders:
Buddhism and Taoism, alongside shamanism and Bon, the
indigenous religion of Tibet; Christianity and Manichaeism,
alongside Islam and Zoroastrianism. It was one of the most
remarkable religious and cultural melting-pots the world has ever
seen.

And it was out of this swirl of religious ideas and identities that
the goddess Kuan Yin first emerges. Where did she come from?
From the need in popular Buddhism for a goddess to compensate
for the male-dominated nature of the faith; from the need to
compete with the Taoists and their successful goddesses, such as
the Queen Mother of the West; from the need for a divine
feminine aspect in faith; and from the interaction between
Buddhists already inspired by the compassionate image of Kuan
Yin, helper of mothers, found in the Lotus Sutra, and Nestorian
Christians bearing images of their Mother of Christ, the Madonna.

The Christian aspect does of course have its own fascinating story.
For the figure of the Madonna, especially holding a child, was
itself taken from the Egyptian statues of the goddess Isis and her
divine child Horus – yet another example of how the divine
feminine, once in a culture, is rarely fully suppressed but
re-emerges in new forms.

So it was on the edge of China that Isis/Mary/Mother of Christ
met the tradition of Avalokitesvara/Kuan Yin who could become
female when necessary and who, as the child-bearer, answered
prayers for children.

This creation of a female Kuan Yin was revolutionary. The
Chinese took basic ideas surrounding a male deity, albeit an
androgynous one with 'feminine' attributes such as compassion,
and turned this around to make the deity female. They created
entirely new forms of statues, unlike anything which had
previously been seen in China (for the statues of the Queen
Mother of the West are severe and distant), remarkable for their

depiction of a gentle, feminine deity. Such revolutionary developments do not drop from the sky! They emerge from interaction with models which supply ideas and stimulus. It is clear that one of the stimuli in the emergence of Kuan Yin's images was the encounter with statues or paintings of Mary.

This was far from the only time that Christian and Buddhist interacted in China. In the year AD 782, the Emperor issued an official communiqué ordering a Christian priest and Buddhist monk to stop working together! An Indian monk by the name of Prajna had recently arrived in the capital Chang-an. He wished to translate a Buddhist scripture into Chinese (the *Ta sheng li ch'u po lo to ching*), and found that the main person he could work with on this was a Chinese Christian priest called Ching Ching, famous for his translation of Christian texts from Syriac and Persian into Chinese. Together they worked on the translation, but unfortunately the end result was not very good as Ching Ching did not understand Sanskrit and Prajna did not understand Chinese! So the Emperor commanded that Ching Ching stick to Christian texts and Prajna to Buddhist so as not to confuse the two faiths.

This illuminating story illustrates how Christians and Buddhists were working together at the most senior level (it is believed Ching Ching was a bishop) in the imperial city. It is easy to imagine that out on the borders of the empire, such interaction was even closer.

This can be seen in the remarkable scroll-painting of a Christian saint, now hanging in the British Museum. It was found, along with a number of Christian texts, in amongst the Buddhist, Manichaean and Taoist texts stored in the caves at Tun Huang, and dates from the ninth century or so. It shows what at first sight looks like a Bodhisattva. Closer examination, however, reveals that it is a Christian saint, for the cross hangs around his neck, is emblazoned on his head-dress and is affixed to the top of a staff he carries. Yet he looks for all the world like a Buddhist Bodhisattva.

When the Portuguese and Spanish Jesuits arrived in China in the late sixteenth century, they brought with them the classic late Renaissance statues of the Madonna. When the Chinese artists and porcelain-makers of Fukien saw these, they immediately recognized their Kuan Yin and began to make models of her which were almost identical to the Spanish and Portuguese Madonna statues. This form of model is the most popular image of Kuan Yin to this day.

We have in Kuan Yin the penultimate stage of a journey of the divine feminine, which began in Egypt with Isis and ended in Japan with the Japanese version of Kuan Yin, Kannon.

While we have to hunt around for clues as to how the Chinese turned the male Kuan Yin into the female, in Japan there is no such difficulty – at least mythologically. The Japanese actually have a legend, set 'historically' in the early eighth century, which describes a deliberate action by the Empress Komyo when she made a female version of the male Kuan Yin/Kannon *(see pages 47–8)*. But for the Chinese, the development of the female Kuan Yin is almost a source of embarrassment – hence the monastic belief that when Kuan Yin enters Nirvana, she will revert to male form. No such tradition exists in Japan.

The Spread of the Worship of Kuan Yin

From her original place of inspiration and development in northwest China, sometime in the seventh to eighth century, Kuan Yin began to spread out across China in her female form. By the tenth century, it is unusual to find a male Kuan Yin except in copies of sutras where the male or androgynous form persists, and by the start of the twelfth century, major centres linking Kuan Yin to stories of earlier goddesses and heroines had begun to emerge.

From the ninth century onwards, Kuan Yin in her female form spread right across China and into Korea and Japan. As she travelled she absorbed all sorts of other female deities, often local deities such as sea goddesses or mountain spirits.

The increasing centralization and consolidation of China under the T'ang and Sung led to the importance of having national religious structures. Taoism offered such an umbrella structure, as did popular Buddhism. Both faiths picked up and absorbed ancient local deities both male and female, offering them positions within the respective celestial or hellish hierarchies of the faith. Many of these deities were aboriginal deities belonging to peoples who were absorbed by the relentless southward push of the Han people. To this day the People's Republic acknowledges 64 aboriginal peoples, though there are in fact many more. It was from peoples such as this that came many of the sea goddesses or mountain or childbirth goddesses who were incorporated into the spreading cult of Kuan Yin.

As this happened, her already diverse sources of origin took on Taoist and even shamanistic hues, making her identity as a purely Buddhist deity in China somewhat inaccurate. For Kuan Yin's success in China is precisely that she transcends barriers of specific religious nomenclature. She is as likely to be found on a Taoist Sacred Mountain as she is on a Buddhist one. Perhaps this is one reason why scholars of Chinese Buddhism have tended to ignore her – because she is so religiously 'promiscuous' – that and the lack of any specific school based around her.

Kuan Yin's appeal is that she responds to the heartfelt needs of ordinary people. She does not impart any great new philosophical truth, nor lead the initiate into deep mysteries of meditation. She is accessible to the most ordinary and the most lowly. She is the friend you call upon in times of trouble. She is the hand that guides. She understands the longing for children, the fear of pain, the anguish of a lost child or of a lonely parent. She is familiar and she is family. It is in this that the strength of Kuan Yin lies – and all this is based upon her basic attribute of compassion, derived, as ever, from the Lotus Sutra.

Wherever you go in the Chinese world, be it mainland China, Taiwan, Hong Kong or the Chinese in diaspora, you will find Kuan Yin. Furthermore, you will find stories told by people of all ages and backgrounds of encounters with the Goddess of Compassion – healing, miracles of deliverance from imminent disaster, guidance at times of stress and anxiety. Kuan Yin is sought as the bringer of children and loved as the embodiment of compassion in a harsh world. Even in the depths of the most rabid anti-religious persecutions in Communist China, she still held a special place. One of the first new statues to a deity erected in China at the tail end of the Cultural Revolution was a massive statue to Kuan Yin in the forecourt of the maternity hospital in southern Canton.

In Part Two I tell some of the key stories of Kuan Yin. These
cover the major strands which flowed into her mythology over
the centuries, such as the story of Miao Shan, the best known
of the legends describing how she came to be. In brief, this
central story relates that she was born as Miao Shan, the third
daughter of a king of ancient China. The king wants to marry
her off but she refuses, saying she wishes to be a Buddhist nun
– she was already noted for her piety and compassion.
Eventually the king agrees to her entering a nunnery but orders
that her life be made as difficult as possible. When this fails to
dissuade her, he sends his army to burn down the nunnery and
kill her. She survives and is whisked away by the gods to a
remote mountain where she perfects herself through
meditation and is joined by her two assistants, a boy and a girl.

Meanwhile, her father falls dangerously ill and is told that the
only medicine that can cure him has to be made from the eye
and arm of a living person without anger. The king is told

that such a person exists and a messenger goes to find her. It is of course his daughter. She willingly gives both her eyes and both arms. The king is healed and comes to pay homage to the one who made such a sacrifice for him. To his horror he discovers it is the very daughter he has sought to kill. He is of course converted to Buddhism and rules as a just king, while Miao Shan ascends to Heaven as the goddess Kuan Yin.

This synopsis will help explain the next stages of the development of Kuan Yin.

I want to turn now to the spread of her worship over the 1,000 years since her emergence onto the wider scene in the ninth and tenth centuries AD.

Unusually for such a deity, we have a fairly good idea how the worship of Kuan Yin spread and where its major centres were, and to some degree still are.

HANGCHOW

In the year AD 939, in a Buddhist monastery in urban and urbane Hangchow on the east coast of China, a monk called Tao I was sitting meditating when he saw a strange glowing light coming from a nearby stream. Going to see what was causing this, he found a piece of beautiful wood, some two feet (0.6 m) long and giving off a rare fragrance. Hauling the piece from the stream, he gave it to a famous local sculptor called Kung, whom he asked to carve it into a statue.

Kung took the piece to his workshop and split the wood open. He found inside a perfectly formed statue of the female Kuan Yin. This is, I believe, the first actual mention we have in Chinese records of a statue of a female Kuan Yin. Certainly it was considered of sufficient newness as an idea for it to need further authenticity from a set of strange dreams in which a white-robed woman appeared and commanded that the statue be worshipped.

Within a short period of time the statue had become famous and pilgrims streamed to Hangchow and to the monastery of Shang Tien Chu to venerate it.

What is intriguing about this story is the fact that for a statue of the female (almost certainly white-robed) Kuan Yin to be accepted at this particular time in China, far from her homeland of northwest China, it had to have a miraculous manifestation and to be guaranteed authentic by visions and dreams.

This period, the very end of the T'ang dynasty and the beginning of the Sung, saw the foundation of many Kuan Yin temples, the production of Kuan Yin miracle books and the flowering of artistic representations of the goddess which have remained important to this day.

In Hangchow, Kuan Yin's rise to fame was assisted by her role in averting disasters and in answering prayers. When Hangchow became the capital city of the Southern Sung (AD 1127–1279) she was lauded by Emperors and high officials alike, while poets strove to praise her. Even when Hangchow lost its role as a capital city, Emperors of the Yuan, Ming and Ch'ing dynasties still offered her praise and funding. Every year from at least the fifteenth century onwards, the feast day of Kuan Yin (the nineteenth day of the second month of the Chinese calendar) was the occasion for a vast temple fair in Hangchow to which hundreds of thousands came.

The story of Kuan Yin in Hangchow is an important one, for the town has always been a favourite centre for the literati and for poets in particular. It was to Hangchow that the highest officials of the Empire liked to retire once they had made their fame and fortune in the courtly circles or in the hierarchies of the bureaucracy. To be appointed to a post in Hangchow was considered to be a sign of great favour.

The significance of these details for this book is that we are fairly sure that *100 Prophecies of Kuan Yin*, translated in Part Three, were written for Hangchow's literate society. We would date them, as an edited collection, to the fifteenth century or thereabouts, though they contain materials from probably the twelfth century onwards. This fits in well with the growth of Kuan Yin-centred activities, such as the annual fair, in Hangchow during this time. Furthermore, it is clear from some of the poems that they were aimed at the retired scholar/official, precisely the sort of clientele Hangchow would have offered. We discuss this in greater detail in the third part of the book.

The Monastery at Hsiang Shan

While Kuan Yin manifested herself in a self-made statue as female, in the early tenth century AD in urban, sophisticated Hangchow, and her veneration spread out from there, a further impetus to her popularity and to her mythological development began in the very early twelfth century.

In the year AD 1100 an ambitious official who had been given a minor posting for a few months visited a monastery at Hsiang Shan in his rather obscure prefecture in Honan. The official, Chiang Chih Ch'i, was given a text which the abbot of the monastery claimed had recently been left behind by a mysterious monk visitor. The book claimed to tell the true story of who Kuan Yin was – the princess Miao Shan – and claimed that her main earthly manifestation had taken place on the very site the monastery was built upon. What is important here is that the official, Chiang Chih Ch'i, believed the book to be genuine and had it published as well as inscribed upon tablets of stone and erected in the compound of the monastery. The abbot, probably interested in the financial rewards of having a major religious figure associated with his monastery, promoted the story vigorously.

Within a very short period of time the monastery at Hsiang Shan had become another major centre for Kuan Yin worship, drawing pilgrims to the remote southern part of Honan in unprecedented numbers.

Between them, Hangchow with its statue and Hsiang Shan with its legend rooted the worship of Kuan Yin deeper and deeper into the religious psyche of China. But it was a small island off the coast of China, some 70 miles from the port of Ningpo, that became the greatest centre for Kuan Yin devotion and has remained so to this day, whereas both Hangchow and Hsiang Shan have declined.

The Island of Pu To

The island of Pu To, known as Pu To Shan, Pu To Mountain, rises sharply and dramatically out of the East China Sea, one amongst a number of small islands in the Chusan archipelago, 70 miles from Ningpo. The natural beauty of the island has long been recognized, for its original name was Hsiao Pai Hua Shan, the Small White Flower Mountain.

The island has been a holy or sacred place for at least 2,000 years, for it was originally a Taoist Sacred Mountain, and one of its other names, lasting through most of the T'ang dynasty until the fame of Kuan Yin overcame it, was Mei Tsen Shan, after a famous first century BC Taoist alchemist Mei Fu who retreated to the island to practise his alchemical skills. To this day, the tallest mountain peak at the southern end of the island is still called Mei Tsen Feng.

Another name, Peach Blossom Mountain, also derives from legends associated with another Taoist recluse, also an alchemist, An Chi Sheng, who lived there in the third century BC. He is reputed to have got very drunk one night and to have tried to paint peach blossom on the rock face of the mountain, for reasons that legend does not disclose! It is said that in the right light, the outline of these paintings can still be seen.

By the first century BC, the island was famous as one of the places where the pill of immortality had been created. One traveller in 113 BC even reported meeting An Chi Sheng alive on the island – which would have made him about 150 years old.

The significance of Pu To Shan is that it is believed to be none other than the mystical island of Kuan Yin, Potalaka, which is described in the Buddhist sutra the Buddhavatamsaka Sutra, which is called the *Hua Yen Ching* in Chinese – the Flower Ornament Sutra, as it is often translated into English. The same Prajna whom we heard of earlier working with the Christian monk Ching Ching translated this sutra in the late eighth century to early ninth century.

The Buddhavatamsaka Sutra describes the wanderings of a young man, Sudhana, who is advised by the Bodhisattva Manjushri to travel the world seeking true friends who will help him to enlightenment. This he does, encountering 53 different spiritual masters from as diverse a bag of characters as you could imagine. This sutra has been described as the *Pilgrim's Progress* of Buddhism. The twenty-eighth true friend that Sudhana encounters is the Bodhisattva Kuan Yin, who lives on an island at an 'isolated place at the end of the ocean'. The name of this island is Potalaka.

The popularity of this book in the ninth to twelfth centuries in particular was one of the major stimuli for the worship of Kuan Yin and the 'identification' of Pu To with Potalaka was one of the major reasons for the island becoming a sacred site of the goddess.

Alongside this very popular text, another, somewhat less well-known text also fed into the tradition of an island called Potalaka associated with Kuan Yin. However, this tradition also claimed that the Buddha had visited there. The snappily titled Sutra of the Thousand-Hand and Thousand-Eyed Kuan Yin of the Great Compassionate Heart (*Chien shou, chien yen Kuan Shih Yin Pusa ta pei hsin to lo ni Ching*) was translated at the beginning of the eighth century and depicts Sakyamuni (the Chinese name for Prince Siddharta), Buddha, teaching within the palace of Kuan Yin on Potalaka island. Interestingly enough, both these texts depict Kuan Yin in male form, yet it is the female Kuan Yin who reigns supreme on the actual island of Pu To.

The influence of these tales is shown in the names of places on Pu To. The highest mountain, the majestic peak to the north of the island, is called Buddha Peak in 'memory' of his having taught there. Meanwhile, down on the seashore in one of the caves which are a feature of the southern end of the island lies Sudhana's cave, where he is supposed to have met Kuan Yin and to have sought his/her advice.

The links made between the mythic Potalaka and Pu To only increased the island's fame and reputation. The same process also took place in Tibet. The Dalai Lama is believed to be an incarnation of Avalokitesvara, which is why his palace in Lhasa is called the Potala – a version of Potalaka.

The association of Pu To with Potalaka was also strengthened by numerous apocryphal Buddhist texts produced through the late Ming and into the Ch'ing dynasties (1400 to 1850s), all of which stressed that just by visiting such a sacred site, benefits could accrue to the pilgrim.

It would appear that Pu To Shan began to develop as a serious Kuan Yin centre from the eleventh to thirteenth century. By the fourteenth century it was so well established that it had already eclipsed Hsiang Shan in Honan. Indeed, in most tellings of the story of Miao Shan from the fifteenth century onwards, the mountain to which Miao Shan is plucked from the burning nunnery is no longer Hsiang Shan but Pu To Shan. *(See pages 65–78 for the story.)*

The eclipsing of Hangchow as a centre for Kuan Yin took longer, but a very interesting story is related of a miracle which took place in 1360 and is recounted in the first history of Hangchow written by Sheng Hsi Ming in 1361. He describes how, in 1360, Hangchow had been sacked in the upheavals which marked the dying days of the Yuan dynasty. The monastery of Shang Tien Chu, where the miraculous statue of Kuan Yin was kept, had been destroyed and the statue had disappeared. A reward was offered for its recovery and it was duly found in the ruins. A devout layman paid for this reward and then had the statue carried in procession to a new monastery Hsi Tien. When the statue was installed, a piercing bright light shot from the statue and penetrated into the sky, where it split into three separate beams. One beam shone out in the direction of Pu To island, one pointed to the old monastery site of Shang Tien Chu and the third pointed down to the new monastery of Hsi Tien. In this way Kuan Yin showed where the three most important centres of her devotion were.

By the late fourteenth century Pu To Shan had become the most important devotional centre of Kuan Yin, eclipsing even Hangchow, and so it remains to this day. As well as being a major centre of Kuan Yin worship, Pu To Shan counts as one of the four Buddhist Sacred Mountains of China (alongside the older five Taoist Sacred Mountains of China).

The central site on Pu To Shan is the Cave of the Tidal Sound, which is where Kuan Yin has often been sighted by devout pilgrims. Such has been the fervour created by this cave that people have often gone to great lengths to try and invoke a sighting of the goddess. One particular form of action was to burn the fingers of each hand, thus illustrating disregard for the worldly and physical in preference to the spiritual and mystical. The story of the mutilation of Kuan Yin in her form as Miao Shan led credence to this particular approach and seems to have been at least one of the main sources of inspiration for this type of religious extremist behaviour. Religious fervour also led many over the centuries to commit suicide in or near the cave, presumably as a means of going into the nether world in the supportive arms of

Kuan Yin. So great a problem did this become that a special temple pavilion was built beside the cave called The Place of No Suicide, in an attempt to add a religious encouragement to preserving life.

The fame of the cave comes from countless stories of sightings and miracles, but the earliest one seems to date from 1080. An embassy was on its way from Hangchow to Korea by ship when it ran into a terrible storm near Pu To. In the midst of the storm a vast turtle rose from the depths and beached the ship in the midst of the sea, making it impossible for it to move. It looked as if the ship and the embassy were doomed, when the leader of the party knelt down facing Pu To and prayed to Kuan Yin to save them. From the dark recesses of the Cave of the Tidal Sound came a golden light. The light grew and grew in intensity and from the cave came the goddess, drifting across the waters. As she emerged she took on the form of the full moon. At such a sight, the turtle dived down into the depths again and the storm abated, allowing the ship to sail on.

When the ambassador returned safely from Korea, he reported
this miracle to the Emperor, who granted imperial recognition and
funds to the main monastery on Pu To, the first time such favour
was shown.

Even making the journey to Pu To Shan could lead to extremes of
religious behaviour. It was not uncommon for monks to make
journeys of over 1,000 miles (often from the Buddhist Sacred
Mountain furthest west, O Mei Shan), kowtowing all the way and
arriving in a dreadful state of bruises, cuts and blood.

The island has been through a terrible series of ups and downs.
From over 300 temples in the late fifteenth century it was reduced
to just one by the 1540s, due to piracy and weak local defensive
forces. But because of the particular devotion of the Emperor Wan
Li (reigned AD 1573–1620) and his mother the Empress Dowager
Li, the monasteries and temples were rebuilt and greatly enlarged.

At the time of the Communist victory and declaration of the
Communist State in 1949, there were 218 temples on the island
with over 2,000 monks and nuns. Most of these survived until the
Cultural Revolution – 1966–1975. Then the island was sacked,
most of the temples destroyed and the monks and nuns driven off
the island. Some have now been allowed to return and novices are
arriving to take up their vocations, but in greatly reduced numbers
and strictly controlled by the State as to how many may live at the
two main monasteries.

Pu To continues to be a centre of pilgrimage but struggles
against the tide of tourism – mostly Chinese – which threatens to
swamp this island of peace and beauty and to disturb one of the
features noted by all visitors down the centuries: the abundance
of wildlife on the island which lives in peaceful co-existence with
the pilgrims, monks and nuns, protected by the sacredness of
the island and the gentleness of its goddess.

In Pu To, the cult of Kuan Yin reaches its apogee, and it is perhaps
no accident that for hundreds of years pilgrims climbing up to the
Buddha Peak Monastery, or the Northern Monastery, as it is also
called, would pass over a great fishpond at the foot of the monastery
buildings and, with their eyes fixed upon the vast Kuan Yin statue
on the upper terrace, would pass a little squat temple – the temple
of the Queen Mother of the West, most definitely in a subordinate

position. For on this former Taoist mountain, Kuan Yin has triumphed.

Pu To Shan is not the only place of worship for Kuan Yin. All the other eight Sacred Mountains of China have their Kuan Yin shrines, though they are not usually the centre-piece of such mountains. Thus, for example, Sung Shan, one of the five Taoist Sacred Mountains and a centre of pilgrimage for those wanting male heirs, has a mass of shrines of Kuan Yin the child-bearer. But it is to Pu To that most pilgrims will turn.

Today the sacred island of the goddess is ablaze with neon, resounds to karaoki and disco bars and has become a major place of prostitution. It is as if the secular has declared war on the divine feminine. This is not the work of Communism but the consequence of the pursuit of consumerism. This seems to be the lowest ebb the sacred island has ever reached and we fear for the future of this unique place. Maybe Kuan Yin will have to perform a miracle on her own island – for little else seems possible in the face of such denigration.

THE BIRTH OF HAN SHAN

It is clear that by the sixteenth century Kuan Yin was firmly established as the major deity of China. From a male deity of the T'ang dynasty, she had emerged through the tenth to sixteenth centuries as a major new spiritual force in the religious landscape – both figurative and literal – of China. Her following had established centres of worship and pilgrimage. Her compassion, her role as sea goddess, her bringing male offspring had all added to her growing fame. By the sixteenth century, Kuan Yin had usurped all the other major deities and had become what she is to this day, that is, the most popular deity of China. Her influence spread from the Emperor to the lowliest peasant and from the pious layfolk to the most renowned monks.

The story of the great Ch'an Buddhism master Han Shan Te Ch'ing (1546–1623) exemplifies the way Kuan Yin penetrated and affected so many aspects of religious life in China.

Han Shan's mother had long wanted a child. Being a devotee of Kuan Yin, she visited her local temple and made offerings before the statue of the White Clad Kuan Yin which resided there. One night she was asleep in bed when she dreamed that a white clad goddess stepped into her room leading a little boy by the hand. A few days later she found she was pregnant and in due course Han Shan was born. As soon as he emerged from the womb, he was wrapped in a white cloth to symbolize his being dedicated to Kuan Yin and to show that he was under her protection.

This protection was soon needed, for when he was about a year old, Han Shan fell dangerously ill. His mother was desperate and prayed night and day to Kuan Yin. When it seemed certain that he would die, she promised that if he lived, he would become a monk. Her prayers were again answered and Han Shan recovered. His mother kept her promise and Han Shan went on to become one of the greatest reforming monks of the Ming dynasty. In particular he combined Ch'an disciplines with Pure Land popular Buddhism, creating a trend which profoundly influenced the state of Buddhism in the late Ming and through into the Ch'ing dynasty.

Perhaps it would be fitting to finish this section, where we have looked at the rise of the devotion to Kuan Yin and in particular the development of her island, by quoting the words of this monk, a monk born as a result of prayers and a dream of Kuan Yin, saved from premature death by the goddess and then dedicated to her.

You don't have to go to the East Sea to meet Kuan Yin.
Pu To is in your mind.

Images of Kuan Yin

I want to turn now to the various forms that Kuan Yin takes and the roles associated with these forms. For Kuan Yin has many titles and many manifestations.

THE WHITE CLAD KUAN YIN

Probably the most famous and widespread image is that of the White Clad Kuan Yin. This image appears to date from the earliest centuries of the goddess's development and pictures her in the simplest of poses and clothes. In its most pure form, for example in Sung dynasty sculpture, Kuan Yin sits draped in white, sometimes with her right leg raised upon her left. Her head is often covered and her cloak flows to the ground, covering her completely. In one hand she usually has a rosary – a symbol which appears in almost all the female forms of Kuan Yin. In the other she holds either a sutra, usually thought to represent the Lotus Sutra, or a vase. The Lotus Sutra refers back to the origin of her powers and compassion. The vase symbolizes her pouring out her compassion upon the world. It is also usual for her to be seated or standing upon a lotus flower, or to have such a flower in her hand or nearby. The lotus is of course one of the most important of Buddhist symbols. It stands for the flowering of the mind and being freed from the murk of this world. For just as the lotus flower is rooted in the mud and dank waters of the pool but flowers only in the light, so through Buddhist teachings can the individual reach enlightenment, especially if helped by a compassionate Bodhisattva.

In this style as the White Clad Kuan Yin, the goddess is serene beauty and compassion incarnate, the white symbolizing purity, unusually for China, for white is usually the colour of death. Some have claimed that as Kuan Yin saves from the cycle of rebirth, she is able to transform the white cloth of mourning and death into the cloak of immortality.

In her mode as White Clad Kuan Yin, she comes very close indeed to the classic Virgin Mary-type statue and, as I have already noted, when the artists of sixteenth-century China saw Spanish Madonnas, they were convinced this was Kuan Yin and proceeded to mass-produce what has become the most common form of Kuan Yin in modern times, the white porcelain Kuan Yin.

Another similarity with the Virgin or Mother of God appears in those statues which depict Kuan Yin as the child giver. The statues of her as a child-bearer vary enormously. Sometimes they are simply a variation of the White Clad Kuan Yin. In such instances, she usually has a child with her, either in her arms or running beside her, normally a boy, this being what most Chinese families wanted – and still want! She is invariably accompanied by her rosary, though sometimes this will be in the beak of a bird which flies above her, serving her, and she also has her willow branch and the Lotus Sutra. Beside her often stand her two helpers, Shan Ts'ai and Lung Nu, the Heavenly Brother and Sister, who joined Kuan Yin during her travails as Miao Shan *(see pages 73–5)*.

The Willow Branch Kuan Yin

Still within the basic form given by the White Clad Kuan Yin is her role as the Willow Branch Kuan Yin.

The willow branch is an important Chinese symbol of Buddhist virtues. It is renowned for its ability to bend in the most ferocious winds and storms and to spring back into shape again. The 'weeping' willow also symbolizes the compassionate concern for the ills of this world which are exemplified in the Mahayana teachings of Buddhism, most notably in the Lotus Sutra. The willow is also an ancient Chinese symbol of femininity and as such was naturally ascribed to Kuan Yin, who is often pictured with what is known as a willow waist.

But the willow also has magical powers. It is used in exorcisms, for it is believed that demons cannot bear the presence of the willow. Interestingly, it is also a key element in shamanistic practices and a means by which the shaman in China can make contact with the spirit world. For all these reasons, it has become one of the key symbols of Kuan Yin.

THE THOUSAND-ARMED, THOUSAND-EYED KUAN YINS

These images are truly extraordinary. In some cases Kuan Yin will literally have 1,000 arms and hands, and in the centre of each hand there is an eye.

There are two somewhat different stories of why she is depicted thus. The most common is that it represents her all-embracing compassion for the world and her constant gaze upon the suffering of all. For this, 1,000 arms and eyes is just sufficient. However, there is a second story which I have heard enough times in different settings to think it worth telling!

According to this variation, when Kuan Yin lived upon Earth in her form as Miao Shan, the king's daughter *(see pages 75–7)*, and had cured her father's illness by offering up both her arms and eyes, her father ordered a statue to be made of her. Wishing to emphasize the sacrifice that she had made, he ordered that the statue be made bereft of eyes and arms.

In Chinese the sound for 'bereft' or 'deficient' and for 'thousand' are virtually identical. At some stage in the transmission of the message to the sculptor, these two words became confused. For months the sculptor worked away, desperately seeking some way to capture imaginatively in stone the wish of the king for a statue of a goddess with 1,000 eyes and 1,000 arms!

At last the grand day of unveiling came. With immense pride the sculptor brought the statue to the palace and the king came to unveil it. Imagine his surprise at finding that, far from having no eyes and arms, Kuan Yin now had 1,000 of each!

In fact, most Thousand-Armed, Thousand-Eyed Kuan Yins have slightly fewer than that – anywhere from 30 to 50. This is because of various mathematical formulae which enable the figure of 1,000 to be reached. For example, many statues will have 40 arms, for each arm is capable of saving 25 worlds or timespans, thus making 1,000. Other combinations of numbers will relate to the various symbols associated with Kuan Yin. In China, 42 hands are frequently shown, each holding a symbol. In Japan the number 38 is most common, again holding various symbols.

The most common such symbols range from those we have already encountered, such as the willow branch, the lotus, the Lotus Sutra and the rosary, through the thunderbolt of enlightenment, a statue of the Buddha and the axe for cutting free from attachments, to the divine creatures of the sun – a crow – and the moon – a rabbit. Each symbol reminds the worshipper of the powers and compassion not just of Kuan Yin but of Buddhism itself. They are visual representations of the teachings of Buddhism and draw us back more than many other statues of Kuan Yin do to the Bodhisattva origins of the goddess and to her roots in Buddhist philosophy and teachings.

KUAN YIN OF THE SOUTHERN OCEAN

Yet another popular style is that of Kuan Yin of the Southern Ocean or Sea. Here the slender form of the White Clad Kuan Yin is combined with swirling waters, leaping fish or placid seas. I have already mentioned the way in which Kuan Yin absorbed the more ancient sea goddesses as she spread eastward away from the high mountains of northwest China to the coasts. The stories linking her to the seas, especially to the seas around Pu To Shan, are multitudinous and the Southern Seas Kuan Yin is a very popular image to this day. It can often be seen in the homes, shops and workplaces of those Chinese who have migrated from the coastal regions of China, such as Shanghai, Hong Kong or Canton. For to these people, it is as protectress on the seas that Kuan Yin is most important.

PROTECTOR OF ALL LIFE

Kuan Yin is frequently pictured standing with a peacock, for, again, her role as protector of all creatures is one which is stressed time and time again in popular legend, song and theatre, as in the creation story given in Part Two. The protection afforded to all creatures on Pu To and in the seas around the island was frequently commented upon by visitors in the past – and devotion to Kuan Yin is often linked to taking up a purely vegetarian diet. Chinese lay

Buddhism is not in essence vegetarian. But devotion to Kuan Yin often carries with it the assumption that you will be mostly if not wholly vegetarian. Statues of Kuan Yin and a peacock remind us of her role as protector of all life and of the Buddhist teachings about the importance of all lives, in whatever form or shape.

This aspect of Kuan Yin's role is the basis for another of her forms. In this shape she rides upon a strange creature which looks a bit like a lion but is called a hou. In this guise she is ruler of the Earth, as its protectress and guardian.

Armed Kuan Yin

A form which rather surprises some from the West is that of the Armed Kuan Yin. In these depictions, Kuan Yin looks like a rather overloaded medieval warrior, clutching and firing a crossbow, bow and arrow and carrying a fierce-looking shield.

This, however, represents Kuan Yin's role as protectress and combatant in the struggle against evil, demons and ignorance. The Chinese Buddhist world of popular belief is infused with evil spirits, devils, ghosts and other beings opposed to the well-being of humans. To protect them from such forces, the Armed Kuan Yin comes riding to their rescue. But at a deeper level, these same weapons are used to symbolize the need to kill off the powers within one's self which restrict the ability of the soul to rise above the material and mundane and reach towards the light of salvation offered by Kuan Yin.

Kannon – The Japanese Goddess

Having traced something of the influence and role of Kuan Yin in China, it is important to move on, for Kuan Yin did not stop there. Both Korea and Japan hold her dear under the name of Kannon. In this section I want to look at the extraordinary journey that Kannon has made in Japan.

Kuan Yin in both male and female form came to Japan in the seventh to ninth centuries when pilgrims to China returned with Buddhist teachings and scriptures, key amongst which was the Lotus Sutra.

Buddhism first appears in the Japanese annals around the middle of the sixth century AD. It was officially introduced at court as part and parcel of the civilization being imported almost wholesale from China via Korea. At the court, an early and powerful convert was Prince Shotoku (574–622). He is often called the Father of Japanese Buddhism, not just because he supported it financially and politically, but because he also wrote commentaries on three sutras, first of which was the Lotus Sutra. Thus right at the very start of Buddhism in Japan, the Lotus Sutra, with its wonderful vision of the compassionate Avalokitesvara, by then already translated into Chinese as Kuan Shih Yin and now transferred to Japanese as Kannon, was present.

Interestingly, when the great medieval statue of Prince Shotoku, which resides in the oldest Buddhist temple complex in Japan (founded by Prince Shotoku in AD 607), was X-rayed recently during renovations, it was found to have another statue built into its centre. Further explorations revealed that the core of the statue of Prince Shotoku was none other than a statue of Kannon. This would seem to imply that Prince Shotoku was considered to be an incarnation of Kannon because of his actions in introducing not just Buddhism to Japan, but especially the Lotus Sutra.

Kannon's rise to fame in Japan mirrors that of Kuan Yin in China, both in terms of scale and historical span. While Kannon has never achieved the supremacy that Kuan Yin has, she has become one of the four or five major deities venerated and respected throughout Japan.

The Thousand-Armed, Thousand-Eyed Kannon is very popular in Japan. In Kyoto, at the Sanjusangen-do Temple, built in 1164, there are in fact 1,000 of these, ranked in serried rows to the left and right of a vast Kannon central

statue. The images are all male, though female figures were by then very common.

What is also interesting in Japan is the tradition that Kannon has had 33 major manifestations. The 33 manifestations are deemed to be major interventions by Kannon in both human and animal forms, both male and female, throughout the endless kalpas of time, in the cycle of worlds that have been, are and will be. They are similar in notion to the idea of the ten avatars of Vishnu in Vedic thought. Indeed, Japanese scholarship claims that the idea and the number came originally from India and the inclusion of certain Vedic/Hindu deities in the 33 seems to bear this out.

The number 33 arises from belief in three distinct worlds: the world of Heaven, the world of the sky and the world of the Earth. Each of these worlds has 11 deities who protect it, thus giving a total of 33. This is fused to an understanding of the Lotus Sutra and in particular the Avalokitesvara chapter, where it is claimed Avalokitesvara/Kuan Yin/Kannon promises to save souls from 33 forms of tribulation.

In a magnificent thirteenth or fourteenth-century silk painting now hanging in the Tokyo National Museum, the 33 manifestations are all portrayed, 16 on each side of a central figure of Kannon in female form. Amongst the 32 manifestations, the majority are female, ranging from nuns to laywomen, while three are in the forms of creatures – a snake, a winged bird-like being and a dragon – each being a form of Kannon. Alongside familiar images such as the White Clad Kannon holding her willow and pot and bringing healing to the world are Karura (based upon the Indian mythological bird Garuda), who symbolizes Kannon as the destroyer of evil, and Ryushin Kannon (snake Kannon) who links the spiritual and physical worlds and can travel across unimaginable distances and times. Yet others depict various forms of the female Kannon, such as the Water Moon Kannon, or a male form, such as the Virtue King Kannon.

The number 33 in relationship to Kannon is central to Japanese thought. For example, there is a pilgrimage route with 33 shrines to Kannon which pilgrims still travel today,

often crawling, as pilgrims of old did in China on their way to Pu To Shan.

The development of these 33 manifestations of Kannon seems to be unique to Japan, for while China has the various symbols associated with Kuan Yin, it has nothing like the belief in these specific manifestations. In China, the various forms of Kuan Yin are seen as more symbolic, whereas Japan seems to have elevated them to a higher system of incarnations.

This fits in with the general Japanese attitude that Kannon incarnates herself quite often in different ways. Whereas China has its Miao Shan stories and then really lets go of any idea of an incarnational experience of Kuan Yin, leaving her to be a vision or a dream or to appear in one of her standard forms, Japan, as would seem to be indicated by the statue inside the statue of Prince Shotoku, believes Kuan Yin can manifest herself in different human forms.

For example, the greatest of the early artists of embroidery was a Buddhist nun called Chujo Hime who came from an important aristocratic family. Her family, especially her stepmother, treated her cruelly and placed as many obstacles as possible in the way of her desire to be a nun. There are echoes here of the Miao Shan story, but with a 'happier' ending! Chujo Hime entered a nunnery and soon displayed wonderful talents in embroidery – an art form at that time virtually unknown in Japan. Her creations are still preserved in the temple of Taema-dera in Yamato. What is significant about her for our story is that she is considered an incarnation of Kannon.

Japan also has two other distinctive forms of Kannon. In China there is a three-headed Kuan Yin, symbolizing the way in which she looks out over all parts of the world simultaneously. In Japan there is an 11-headed Kannon. Surmounting the main head are a row of four heads on each side of the crown of the main head, with a larger one on the very top and a slightly larger one at the back. In some statues, the faces on one side of the head are all male and rather fierce, while the faces on the other side are female and more benign. However, there seems to be considerable regional variation in this. But again the notion seems to be that Kannon looks out over all the world, sometimes having to be stern and severe, sometimes compassionate and gentle. What I like best of all about these statues is that the slightly larger head at the back is almost always laughing!

One very strange style is almost always male and frequently of fierce visage. This is the Horse-Headed Kannon. Again, in Chinese art there are pictures of Kuan Yin with a horse attendant, called the Horse Voice Kuan Yin. But in Japan, Kannon is pictured with three heads surmounted by a horse's head. The belief is that this style relates back to India and to the cult of the horse there. This involved releasing a white stallion at New Year and then the tribe or clan following wherever the horse wandered, taking this to be divine guidance for conquest or resettlement. In Japanese thought, Kannon wanders the world combating evil and ignorance. But this version of Kannon is also believed to deliver you from a bad rebirth in the next life. It prevents you coming back as an animal.

However, it is as Koyasu Kannon that the Japanese goddess is most popularly represented – Kannon of the Easy Delivery – the child-bearing Kuan Yin of China. A very interesting legend relates to the Japanese version of this – interesting because of its links to Shintoism, of which more shortly, but also because it shows clearly the understanding within Japanese Buddhism that the change of Avalokitesvara from a male to female form was a conscious shift. It is also helpful in dating when this shift began to take shape.

The Empress Komyo (AD 710–60) had fallen pregnant and was very anxious to have an easy and safe delivery. Being very worried and distressed about this, she prayed fervently to the Shinto goddess and founder of the Imperial Family, Amaterasu, for an easy birth. One night, Avalokitesvara in male form came to her in her dreams and stood beside her bed. When the Empress awoke she found a small statue of the Bodhisattva on her bed. She had this statue with her as she gave birth and sure enough, it was a very easy delivery. Afterwards she had the statue encased within a vast Thousand-Armed Kannon and placed in a new temple she founded in Kyoto, called the Taisan-ji Temple. This is still a very popular temple for women.

What is very interesting is that up to this point in the story Kannon is still male – including the Thousand-Armed Kannon. But, the legend continues, the Empress then ordered a statue to be made of the Kannon of Easy Delivery, holding a child, but modelled upon the Empress herself and therefore female. This version of the statue then became immensely popular.

The story is interesting for a number of reasons, but its greatest significance lies in the obvious need to explain how the male Avalokitesvara came to have a female, child-carrying version. The date is also interesting. The story is obviously apocryphal and is acknowledged to be so by Japanese Buddhist monks. Yet it reflects the fact that in the ninth to tenth centuries, the Japanese found the female Kuan Yin statues in China and began to bring them to Japan, confusing people who were already accustomed to the male form and necessitating this legend. This is yet another indicator of the immense shift in thinking which the creation of the female Kuan Yin/Kannon marked.

But let me finish this journey to Japan and into the beliefs about Kannon with one further, somewhat extraordinary development.

Kannon, like Kuan Yin, crosses religious boundaries. She is beloved of both Buddhists and Shintos in Japan. Her compassion means she transcends boundaries, though in Japan boundaries between Buddhism and Shinto are fairly porous to begin with.

This century has seen the most dramatic increase in religious groups in Japan since the twelfth century AD. Many of these New Religious Movements, such as Soka Gakkai and Rissho Kosei Kai, have Buddhist foundations, even if their particular beliefs and practices diverge from what most would know as mainstream Buddhism. In these groups, Kannon has an honoured position.

However, there are some Shinto New Religious Movements. One of these is Sekai Kyusei Kyo, founded by a healer called Mikichi Okada. In the mid 1920s he began a ministry of healing and revelation. At times it has been claimed that he believed himself to be an incarnation of Kannon herself. However, I have been told that this is not strictly true. Rather he believed himself to be a vehicle for her messages to humanity. This Shinto group holds Kannon to be central to its teachings and mission, but their understanding of her is radically different from that which one might expect. For Sekai Kyusei Kyo, following the revelations given by Kannon to Okada, teach that far from being a Buddhist Bodhisattva in origin, Kannon is none other than a Shinto deity who descended to Earth with her sister, the sun goddess Amaterasu.

The story, as told in Okada's own words (and kindly translated for me by order of President Kawai of MOA International), reflects a trend discernible within certain Japanese religious groups where the non-Japanese origin of aspects of their culture causes concern. It is a fascinating example of how Avalokitesvara/Kuan Yin/Kannon continues to exercise and stretch the religious imagination in ways unexpected, even to this day.

Okada, recounts the following:

> . . . when I learned that Kannon's spirit rests by my side at all times, I was of course quite surprised; moreover from the moment of realisation, miracles relating to Kannon began to take place . . . it was as a result of these events that I came to know that Kannon is really a deity called Izunome, and that when a propitious moment arrives, Kannon, who has taken

carnal form for a certain duration in order to save
humanity, will return to Her divine state.[11]

It is immediately interesting to note that whereas most
Chinese Buddhist teachers claim Kuan Yin will return to her
proper form as a man in the fullness of time, Japan has no
problems with this and assumes her true form is female.

Okada goes on to recount that although Kannon in the form
of Izunome originally descended to Earth in Japan, Japan
became spiritually too dangerous and rebellious a place to stay:

> Just at that time the gods of Korea, particularly
> Susano-o, had come to Japan and threatened
> Izunome's position. But Izunome would not yield
> easily, so pressure and persecution worsened, until
> finally Izunome's very life was at stake. Whereupon,
> abandoning Her position, She went into disguise to
> avoid notice and secretly fled from Japan, passing
> through China and eventually on to India. There,
> assuming the name of the bodhisattva Kanjizai,
> Izunome built a new and pristine refuge on Mount
> Ptalaka, a mountain of moderate height on the
> southern coast of India.

Okada goes on to say that Kannon preached here to 28
disciples, giving teachings based upon Shinto truths. The
youthful Buddha heard about these teachings and as a result
of them abandoned his wealth, security and home. Okada
ends this part of his revelation with the words:

> From this we know beyond a shadow of a doubt that the
> true founding patron of Buddhist law was actually
> Izunome, a goddess from Japan.

The revelation goes on to spell out that when preaching to
Indians, Kannon took a male form because they could not
appreciate that true spiritual insight could come from a
woman. Dwelling in India in the 'Age of Night', spiritual
understanding was limited, but as the 'Age of Day' emerged
(some 2,000 or so years ago, claims Okada), Kannon moved
from India to China, where she was able to reveal her true

female form as Kuan Yin. From there she was able to return at last to Japan.

The Appeal of Kuan Yin

Although Kuan Yin's story has undergone transformations over the centuries, what stands out throughout – whether as male Avalokitesvara, male/female Kuan Yin/Kannon or Kannon/Izunome – is that the heart of her appeal is compassion for suffering humanity; indeed, for all suffering life. Even in its wilder versions, the hopeful message of the compassion and mercy, salvation and hope of the Lotus Sutra continues to infuse and inspire devotion to the One who Hears the Cries of the World.

The significance of Kuan Yin lies in a number of different directions. She is significant because, across China, she is loved and venerated more than any other deity, while in Korea and Japan Kannon is one of the most revered deities. She is significant because of her popular appeal – she is a goddess of the poor and the needy. She is significant because of her role in Chinese religious mythology and landscape.

But her greatest significance is as the outpourings or embodiment of the divine feminine. In Kuan Yin we encounter compassion. In a world of spirits, devils, demons, ghosts, maverick deities, angry ancestors and the like, she shines like a divine lighthouse, leading home the lost, the bewildered and the distressed. In her worship, the divine becomes suffused with beauty and grace, with love and mercy, with gentleness and wisdom. In this Kuan Yin stands in stark contrast to most of the other powerful deities of China and

Japan – grim figures such as Kuan Di the god of war; door guardians of Buddhist temples; the anonymous local earth gods; or the terrifying aspects of the kings of the various Buddhist and Taoist hells.

In invoking Kuan Yin, one reaches out to touch the light side, the gentle side of divinity. In seeking her help, her guidance, you hear the softer wisdom of woman amidst the preaching of the Buddhas or the war cries of the combatant deities. To listen to or to gaze upon Kuan Yin is to be calmed, centred and in this way brought to see both your depths and your limitations. In praise of her, great artists of stone, wood, metal and word have sought to create beauty, tranquillity and peace. For the millions around the world who turn to her each day, this is what Kuan Shi Yin, the One who Hears the Cries of the World, the feminine made divine, offers to those who will meet her.

Endnotes

1. All translations of the Lotus Sutra given are taken from W. E. Soothill's translation from the Chinese, published as *The Lotus of the Wonderful Law*, Clarendon Press, Oxford, 1930.
2. Figures quoted from the survey by Tsukamoto in *Buddhist and Taoist Practices in Medieval Chinese Society*, ed. David W. Chappell, University of Hawaii, 1987, page 78
3. See Riane Eisler, *The Chalice and the Blade*, Mandala, London, 1987.
4. See *I Ching*, Palmer, Ramsay and Zhao, Aquarian, London, 1995, Hexagram 35, line two.
5. *Tao Te Ching: The new translation*, Kwok, Palmer and Ramsay, Element Books, Shaftesbury, 1993.
6. Ibid., Ch. 52.
7. Suzanne Cahill, *Transcendence and Divine Passion: The Queen Mother of the West in medieval China*, Stanford University Press, Stanford, 1993, page 13.
8. Shan Hai Ching, *The Classic of the Mountains and the Seas*, 2.19a, quoted on page 16 of Cahill, op. cit.
9. S. T. Cheung in *Kwun Yum*, published by the Tung Wah, Hong Kong, 1983, page 3.
10. See pages 95–133 in Palmer, *Living Christianity*, Element Books, Shaftesbury, 1993.
11. Mikichi Okadan, *A Personal Confession* (*Jikan-sosho kiseki-monogatari 4*), 5 October 1949.

2

⊚ ⊚ ⊚ ⊚ ⊚ ⊚ ⊚ ⊚ ⊚

THE MYTHS
AND LEGENDS OF
KUAN YIN

THE MYTHS AND LEGENDS OF KUAN YIN

The myths and legends of Kuan Yin are beyond reckoning. Almost every fervent believer in the powers of the goddess has his or her own story of miraculous intervention. At the great temples where particularly important images of her are situated, there are tales of how the statue was made or found, of the healing it has produced and of the wonders performed by the goddess through the image. In countless legends the goddess appears as the calm, healing and soothing saviour of the situation.

In Chinese tradition there are three major types of Kuan Yin story, each of which has many forms and versions.

Kuan Yin in Creation

These stories are probably amongst the most recent, for the notion of a specific 'Creation' is relatively new in Chinese myth and legend. In these stories, Kuan Yin plays a very significant role. Chinese creation myths do not posit a creator figure, though occasionally the Buddha is seen in such a guise. The traditional Chinese explanation of creation is vague about why and how and tends instead to view creation as the consequence of the coming into being of the two primordial forces, yin and yang. From their existence comes the vital energy and struggle which causes all life to be.

In one popular story of Kuan Yin, she is present from the earliest stages of creation as part of an ill-defined world of gods and goddesses who oversee this world's creation. When the multitude of species (in Chinese literally 'the 10,000 species') are created,

Kuan Yin comes down to Earth to rule over them and to teach each of them how to live.

At the beginning of time, when the world was young and all the creatures of the world but newly made, Kuan Yin dwelt with all the creatures upon Earth. At first she taught them how to live, each according to their own ways. She taught them how to treat others and how to show kindness to their young. Under her tutelage, the animals, birds and insects lived happily together. If a disagreement broke out, they came to her for advice. Thus was all peaceful in the world and every creature loved and adored Kuan Yin.

But the day came when she had to ascend to Heaven again to take up her responsibilities there. The animals, birds and insects were devastated when they heard this. 'Please do not leave us,' they cried, 'for who will teach us and guide us if you are not here?'

Kuan Yin was moved by their pleas and agreed to stay upon the Earth for a little longer. But soon she knew she must return to Heaven and even though the creatures begged her to stay, she sadly had to refuse.

On a bright summer's day, with all the creatures of the world gathered around, she ascended to Heaven upon a cloud, leaving the creatures below heart-broken.

At first they tried to continue as if she was still with them. When arguments broke out they would try and think what she would have said or done. To begin with this sort of worked. But soon the divisions and disagreements became too deep seated. Anger and enmity broke out and animals fell upon each other in ferocious attacks or ran to hide from the stronger creatures.

Soon the woes of the world reached such a peak that Kuan Yin heard their cry for help and mercy. Moved by compassion, she descended to Earth. As soon as she appeared, the various parties in the numerous disputes and arguments came before her and pressed their respective cases. One animal complained of being hunted by another; certain creatures felt they had the right to be able to swim but could not; yet others wanted to be able to fly. Patiently, over the next few weeks Kuan Yin dealt with all the various complaints, proposals and disputes.

At the end of this time she again took her leave and again the creatures implored her not to go. And again, for a while all was calm. But gradually the order she had re-established broke down again. Animal set upon animal; the birds argued over who was most powerful and the insects invaded each others' nests. Uproar engulfed the world and the din reached even to Heaven.

Here Kuan Yin heard the noise and, looking down, saw the confusion. So yet again she descended to Earth. Once more she dealt with the arguments, expectations and frustrations of the creatures. Weeks passed and at last all was sorted out and she again ascended to Heaven – but this time with a stiff warning that all the creatures must learn to deal with their own problems.

But it was not to be! Within a few days the situation was as bad as before. Violence, deceit, falsehood, argument and fear were yet again the order of the day. The wailing and moaning, complaining and dispute of the creatures arose yet again to Heaven, where it disturbed the rest of the gods and goddesses. Turning to Kuan Yin, they asked her to sort the creatures out once and for all.

On her white cloud, Kuan Yin descended to Earth. Within hours, messengers were streaming out from her grotto to all parts of the world, summoning all the creatures to meet her within a week. From far and wide they came, borne upon the tides, riding the winds, traversing the land. Once they were all gathered before her she spoke.

'Oh you 10,000 beings, why do you cause such distress? Why can you not live together? Each of you has your own place and role, so why such envy of others? Why do you not live in peace?'

The creatures hung their heads in shame, unable to think what to say. But then the rabbit spoke up.

'Beloved Kuan Yin, when you are with us, watching over us, we fear nothing. There are no disputes, no envy, no false striving. But once you go, once we feel you have left us alone, then we fall into such bad behaviour. Can you not stay with us?'

At this all the creatures added their voice in supplication that Kuan Yin would never leave them again.

Kuan Yin was deeply moved by their obvious sincerity. But she also knew she had other tasks to undertake which meant she could not always be present upon the Earth. Being compassionate, however, she sought within her heart for some solution.

Suddenly she held up her hand for silence. The ranks of creatures fell silent and waited. Then Kuan Yin beckoned to a large but rather dull-looking bird to come close to her. The main distinguishing feature of this bird was the number and size of his tail feathers. When he stood beside her, she spoke.

'My friends, it is obvious that I cannot be with you at all times. But it is also clear that you need me to watch over you in some way. So I have resolved upon this action.'

So saying, she swept her hands across her face and then cast them over the dull brown feathers of the big bird. Instantly the bird was suffused in exploding colours and lights, so bright that the other creatures had to avert their eyes.

When at last their eyes were able to see again, they could hardly believe what they saw. For on each of the 100 tail feathers of the bird was now a bright clear eye staring back at them. Turning to Kuan Yin, they sought understanding of this transformation.

'My friends,' said the goddess, 'I cannot watch over you at all times in all places. But my servant the peacock can. Each of his eyes will watch over you, guard you and tell me of what is happening in this world. When you see the peacock's 100 eyes you will know that I care for all of you. Let the peacock be my servant in this world and know that I look after you.'

With that she began to rise into the sky, bidding the assembled creatures a fond farewell.

And to this day the peacock struts because of his special role as her servant. And each day the 100 eyes of each peacock look out over the world, reminding all who understand that Kuan Yin watches over them.

This story is, as far as I can find, quite a recent one – by which I mean it does not appear in any records I have seen until the Ming dynasty, *c.* AD 1450. It clearly builds upon the original Sanskrit name of Avalokitesvara, which means, 'The Lord who Regards the Cries of the World'. I suspect that there was an old legend concerning the peacock's eyes and divine protection, which was taken over at some stage by the figure of Kuan Yin as the most obvious candidate for such compassionate concern.

The Princess Miao Shan

The second legend associated with Kuan Yin is the most famous and the one which has most powerfully shaped both the iconography and the popular devotion to her. This is the story of the Princess Miao Shan.

Considerable attention has been paid to this story by scholars over recent years for it is a fascinating legend, not just in terms of its narrative excitement but also because we can date almost to the very day, month and year when it was first conclusively fused to the figure of Kuan Yin. Whether the story of Miao Shan existed long before it was linked to Kuan Yin seems unclear. It has a certain universality about it which would indicate that it was originally a free-standing story and thus may be of considerable antiquity. However, about its existence prior to the year AD 1100 we know virtually nothing. But early in that year a new prefect was appointed to the area of Ju Chou in southern Honan. This relatively quiet backwater was only a temporary post for the official, one Chiang Chih Ch'i. In fact he only spent about one month there, from the end of the previous year to sometime in early February 1100. However, during that time he visited the Buddhist monastery at Hsiang Shan, a small mountain or hill range in his prefecture. Here there was an already well known pagoda dedicated to Ta Pei – the name for the Thousand-Armed Kuan Shi Yin. In this case, the pagoda housed a male statue of Ta Pei which was credited with miraculous powers.

Chiang Chih Ch'i seems to have been greatly impressed and excited by his visit to the monastery and at seeing the Ta Pei statue. But what excited him even more was what he deemed to be his 'discovery' of the original dwelling-place of Kuan Yin in her main earthly manifestation as the princess Miao Shan.

When Chiang Chih Ch'i visited the monastery he was cordially met by the abbot, Huai Chou, who told him of a mysterious visit just that very month by a strange monk who had suddenly appeared at the monastery and just as mysteriously disappeared again. During his brief visit, he had handed to the abbot a book which he claimed to have found amongst a pile of old books in a monastery on Nan Shan. The book was called *The Life of the Ta Pei Bodhisattva of Hsiang Shan* and it was the name Hsiang Shan that

had drawn the monk to the monastery there and thus to this encounter with the abbot.

When the strange monk had disappeared, the abbot had read the book and was astonished by the story set out therein. The abbot gave the book to Chiang Chih Ch'i to read and the effect upon the prefect was remarkable. As he read the story he felt that Kuan Yin had specifically brought him to the monastery and to this encounter with the story of her life as princess Miao Shan so that he could use his wealth and prestige to make her story well known. In particular he was struck by a line in the book which prophesied that after 300 years from the date of the composition of the book, there would be a revival in the worship of Kuan Yin. Feeling called and commissioned, he decided to act straightaway. So impressed was he by the story and by his standing on the actual spot where Kuan Yin had lived in human form that he commissioned one of the greatest calligraphers of the age to inscribe a stele with the details of her story engraved upon it. This was duly erected in the monastery grounds.

The effect of this stele and of the story it told was dramatic in the extreme. The monastery began to attract vast hordes of pilgrims who swarmed there to read the stele and to pay homage at such a sacred site.

In his study of this story, Glen Dudbridge[1] makes the case that this so-called mysterious monk and book were deliberately constructed by the abbot to attract the attention of a wealthy patron such as Chiang Chih Ch'i who through his energies would give authority to the story of Kuan Yin's earthly manifestation at Hsiang Shan.

Dudbridge goes on to ask, 'If these reflections prompt us to look doubtfully at the testimony of Huai-chou it is logical to ask what he would have stood to gain by devising such a document and giving it such a background. The answer is: a great deal.'[2]

He goes on to point out that the abbot was already deeply committed to a major programme of renovation and rebuilding. The development of a major sacred pilgrimage site was exactly what he could do with, for the money generated by such centres was immense.

It seems clear from the work of scholars such as Dudbridge, Stein and Tsukamoto that the linking of the story of Miao Shan with Kuan Yin does not date before this particular incident. Thus we can date to almost the exact day when Kuan Yin's most famous story took wings and developed into the major legend which it is to this very day. This is another fascinating example of how Kuan Yin has been constructed by various forces, spiritual and material, over the centuries.

But what of the story? The earliest versions are quite stark and straightforward. Over the centuries, as with any good story, the core has been expanded and embellished. What follows is in essence the main story with some of the major additions included where appropriate.

Long, long ago, over 4,000 years ago, there arose a usurper who overthrew the King of Hsing Lin and took the kingdom for his own. His reign title was Miao Chuang. His queen was called Pao Te and between them they ruled the land. Much as they longed for a son, the gods would not grant them one because of the bloodshed caused by Miao Chuang's usurpation of the throne. Despite the pleas of the king and queen, their ministers and numerous priests and sages, the gods remained firm in their refusal and instead granted the royal pair three daughters. Now some say these daughters were the reincarnated souls of three worthy boys born to a devout Buddhist family who were murdered by brigands. But none can say for sure. What can be told is that Her Royal Majesty gave birth to these three beautiful daughters. The first to be born was called Miao Yen and the second one was called Miao Yin. But it is the last one who is the concern of our story.

At the moment of the conception of this last daughter, Queen Pao Te dreamed she had swallowed the moon. When the child was about to be born, the whole world shook with an earthquake, the air was laden with a most wondrous scent and divine flowers sprang up all across the land. As soon as she came forth from the womb this third daughter, named Miao Shan, was as fresh and clean as if she had been newly washed. Her countenance was of divine beauty and her body was covered by Heavenly clouds of diverse hues. To those who saw her birth there was no doubt that she was a goddess. But her parents, still hoping for a son, were furious and, ignoring these signs of divinity, took against her.

In his disappointment at the lack of a son and heir, the king could only take comfort in the hope of good marriages for his daughters. His chief minister pointed out that through the sons-in-law he was bound to gain through marrying off his three daughters, he would have a choice of three young men to take over his kingdom. So the king and queen set their hopes on the finding of suitable marriage partners for their daughters.

But from an early age, Miao Shan showed that her interests were not those of an ordinary girl. She spent her time in prayer and meditation. She chose to dress in plain and simple cloth, scorning the rich brocades of the court. Her diet was likewise simple, a bowl of rice and vegetables rather than the sumptuous feasts of the royal household. In her behaviour and demeanour she showed, to those who could see, that she was a Bodhisattva. But to her parents and to her sisters, she seemed just odd and difficult.

As she grew to adulthood, her love of charity and kindness earned her the name of Maiden with the Heart of the Buddha. Through her example, her ladies-in-waiting were brought to faith in the Buddha and turned from their frivolous ways towards a more humble and generous spirit.

Let me give you just one example of the compassion of this wonderful child. She was sitting by herself in the garden of the palace one evening. Above her sat a cicada who was happily chattering away. The sound of the cicada gradually lulled her off to sleep. In the midst of her dreams she heard a terrible scream. Waking with a start from her slumbers, she leaped to her feet to see what creature it could be that was in such distress. She saw that the little cicada had been grabbed by a large praying mantis who had wrapped its legs tightly around the little insect.

Desperate to save the creature from the grip of the praying mantis, Miao Shan clambered up onto the wall where she reached out and freed the cicada from the mantis' hold. Angry at being deprived of its prey, the mantis turned on Miao Shan and attacked her hand. Startled by this, Miao Shan lost her footing on the wall and with a cry fell to the ground, cutting her forehead.

Her sisters, hearing her cry out, rushed to her. They found her with blood flowing from the wound on her forehead and sought to comfort her. But Miao Shan merely shrugged her shoulders and said, 'A scar on my forehead is a small price to pay for the life of a cicada.' This is just one example of the generosity of heart which Miao Shan showed every day to all living beings.

But none of this cut any ice with the king and queen! They were not impressed by this gentle soul in their midst and her father determined to find her a husband as soon as he could.

By now the king had already found desirable husbands for his two eldest daughters and great festivities had been held to celebrate their nuptials. Now he was determined to find a suitable young man for Miao Shan. But she had her own ideas – and they did not include marriage. Coming before her royal father, she spoke her mind.

'Riches and fame are not eternal; glory and magnificence are mere bubbles, illusions. I wish to become a nun and to renounce the world. Even if you force me to work as a servant, I shall never change my mind or my resolve.'

Her mother tried to plead with her and brought her again before her father, begging her to reconsider.

To this Miao Shan replied: 'I will do as you command if as a result three troubles of the world are prevented.'

The king was astonished at this and asked her, 'What do you mean by "three troubles of the world"?'

She replied: 'The first trouble is that when people are young their faces are fair as a jade moon, but with old age their hair turns white, their faces wrinkle and whether they are active or passive, they are in every way worse off than when they were young.

'The second trouble is that a person's body may be lithe and trim, fit and healthy. They may walk with ease, moving like a bird on the wing. But should illness strike they collapse into bed, taking no pleasure in anything.

'The third trouble is that someone might have a host of friends and relatives, be always surrounded by companions and those who are dearest. Then comes the day of death and suddenly this is all at an end. Neither friend nor relative can take their place.

'So, if being married can help heal these troubles, then I will willingly give myself in wedlock. If not, then I ask permission to retire to a life of religious devotion.'

Her father was aghast at this and exploded with rage. He stormed at her but to no avail. Her mother, seeing her resolve, took her on one side and tried to argue with her.

'What you ask is impossible. Try and be reasonable. We have chosen a good man as your prospective husband. He is a good military man.'

Miao Shan, seeing the genuine concern of her mother, spoke again.

'Mother, if I must marry then I could only marry a doctor.'

Before she could go any further, her mother exploded with indignation. 'A doctor! A doctor! What sort of prince would such a person make? How could such a person rule? Why a doctor, for goodness sake?'

Miao Shan spoke again quietly. 'My desire is to heal the world of all its ills; of the chills of winter and the heats of summer; of the fires of lust and the damp of old age; of all sickness. I wish to make all equal, regardless of riches and poverty. I want all things to be shared so no one goes without or has more than they need. If I can marry a man who will help me in this, then I shall marry tomorrow.'

Her mother saw that reasoned argument would have no effect upon her and reported the conversation to her husband the king. The king decreed that Miao Shan was to be set to work on the most demeaning jobs in the palace and that she was to be given only just enough food and drink to keep her alive.

Her sisters, seeing her so reduced, pleaded with her to change her mind and marry, but they could not prevail against her resolve to take the religious path. When her mother went to intercede with her again, Miao Shan rebuked her, saying, 'Empty things come to an end. I desire what is infinite.'

Her mother realized nothing could shake her resolve so asked the king to allow Miao Shan to retire to a nunnery and take up the religious life. The king was furious and he decided he would teach her a lesson. He summoned the abbess of the nunnery that Miao Shan had chosen. This was the Nunnery of the White Sparrow, in the prefecture of Ju Chou. He instructed the abbess that while he was prepared to allow Miao Shan to enter the nunnery, he expected the nuns to make life as difficult and unpleasant as possible for the princess, so that she would come to her senses.

Upon her entry into the nunnery, the abbess put Miao Shan to work in the kitchen with instructions that if she did not do well there, she would be dismissed. Such a lowly posting was, of course, exactly what Miao Shan wanted. She set to with a will, but even for her the tasks were demanding ones.

In Heaven, the Master of Heaven saw her labours and the difficulties some of the nuns put in her way out of envy. He called up the god of the North Star and told him to bring the gods of the

Five Sacred Mountains, the Eight Ministers of the Heavenly Dragon and the local Earth gods to her assistance. The Sea Dragon was ordered to dig a well for her and tigers brought firewood while birds collected vegetables for her and the gods summoned to her service toiled in the kitchen at her command.

The result of all this divine help did not go unnoticed in the nunnery. One nun spoke out against Miao Shan, fearful of the king's anger, but the princess rebuked her.

'Have you not heard that those who try to obstruct a monastic vocation will suffer torments for innumerable aeons? Do you willingly oppose the Buddhist faith and accept the risks of retribution in the hells?'

The nun, aghast at this, protested her innocence, saying, 'I am under the king's orders. It is not of my choice.'

Despite such attempts to undermine her resolve, Miao Shan would not give in and get married. Word of all this soon reached the king whose temper finally broke. In a rage he ordered the commander of the palace troops to go immediately to the nunnery and burn it to the ground, killing all the nuns therein.

The commander took a force of over 5,000 hand-picked, ruthless soldiers. Swiftly they moved. Swiftly they surrounded the nunnery. Swiftly they set fire to the surroundings and watched as the flames raced towards the nunnery.

In the nunnery pandemonium broke out, with nuns rushing in all directions. Some found Miao Shan and began abusing her, saying, 'This is all your fault.'

Miao Shan, horrified at what was happening, fell on her knees and prayed to Buddha: 'Great Sovereign of the Universe, I am the daughter of a king. You were the son of a king. Just as you left your palace to seek enlightenment, taking to the remote hills, so have I left my palace and come to this mountain. Please hear my prayer and rescue your younger sister and her fellow nuns.'

So saying, she pricked the top of her mouth and then spat the blood into the air. Instantly it transformed into vast rain clouds which poured down upon the raging fires and quenched them, to the amazement of all who watched. The nuns were safe.

The commander of the palace guards retreated and reported back to the king. The king could stand it no more and ordered that Miao Shan be seized, bound in chains and brought back to the palace to be immediately executed. Without a moment to rest, the commander returned to the nunnery with his troops, seized Miao Shan, bound her hand and foot and bore her off to the palace.

Her mother tried once again to plead with her, but to no avail. The king gave the command that at dawn the next day she was to be executed. But he was overheard by the Earth gods, who reported all this to the Master of Heaven. The Master of Heaven summoned the Earth god of the execution square and told him that he was to use all his magic to prevent any wound being inflicted upon the princess. At the moment of her death he was to transform himself into a tiger and leap out to snatch up her body. He was to bear it away to a safe place, put a pill of immortality in her mouth to prevent her body decaying and then await the return of her soul from its journeys.

The next morning, as dawn broke, the princess was led out into the execution square. As the executioner lifted his sword, a brilliant light fell all around Miao Shan. The executioner's sword shattered into pieces. When he tried to kill her using a spear, the spear dissolved in his hand. Eventually he had to resort to using a silken cord to strangle her.

As her breath died within her, the onlookers scattered in terror as a huge tiger bounded into the square. Roaring and leaping, he covered the square in two bounds, seized the body of Miao Shan in his mouth and was gone before any could move or think.

The Earth god tiger bore Miao Shan's body to a forest where he laid her down and placed the pill of immortality in her mouth.

Meanwhile her soul had begun its journeys. She awoke from her death sleep to find herself in a terrible, desolate place.

'What is this place?' she asked aloud.

She was answered by a tall young man standing beside her who told her she was in the first of the Eighteen Buddhist Hells. The

sights that greeted her of the souls of the damned tortured and tormented beyond belief moved her to profound compassion. She immediately began to pray for those who were in such agony around her. Instantly the hells began to be transformed. The terrible heat gave way to a pleasant climate. The instruments of torture turned into flowers and trees. Hell became in fact, a Paradise and the damned rejoiced at her mercy.

But the Kings of Hell went to complain to the Emperor of Hell. 'For there to be justice in the world, there must be both Heaven and hells. Through the mercy of Miao Shan, the hells are now the same as Heaven. Thus there can be no true justice. We beseech you, release Miao Shan so that the hells can once again become the places of punishment and justice can once again be administered.'

The Emperor of Hell agreed and had Miao Shan escorted back to her body. He gave her a peach of immortality to eat which brought her back to life.

Upon waking, once more alive, Miao Shan found herself on Hsiang Shan and there she dwelt for many years perfecting herself, realizing her full Bodisattva nature. At the end of nine years, all the gods came to greet her and to salute her wisdom. She asked that they find her two companions, a virtuous maiden and a worthy young man.

The gods chose for her a young man who from an early age had devoted himself to religious studies as a hermit monk. When this young man, whose name was Shan Ts'ai, was brought before her, she decided to test his devotion to her. She set him to meditate upon a mountain top near to her. Then she commanded the local Earth gods to take up the disguise of brigands and to storm her part of the mountain top.

Instantly, a savage horde appeared at the base of the mountain and came swarming up, apparently intent upon slaying Miao Shan. Miao Shan, feigning distress, rushed up the mountain and, as she reached the peak, stumbled and fell down the mountain face.

Shan Ts'ai, seeing this happen and giving no thought to himself or his own safety, leaped from his peak, plunging down the deep chasm, until he reached Miao Shan. When he reached her, he rebuked her for such folly and she rebuked him for his impetuousness! Then she asked him to look down to the very bottom of the chasm and tell her what he saw. Looking down, he saw a corpse.

'That is your former body,' said Miao Shan. 'Through your devotion to me, you have been released from your old body and given this immortal body. Now you will be able to walk the clouds, climbing up to Heaven and plunging down to the depths. But from now on you will stay by my side always.'

Bowing low and kowtowing, Shan Ts'ai thanked her from the bottom of his heart and from that day until this, he has never left her side.

Not long after, Miao Shan was scanning the world, which her spiritual vision allowed her to do. Looking deep into the ocean, she saw the third son of the great Water Dragon King. He was swimming through the waters in the form of a vast carp, on an errand for his father. As he did so, he unwittingly fell into the net of a fisherman who hauled him up and set off for the market. Miao Shan, seeing his distress and predicament, sent Shan Ts'ai to the market with a vast fortune to purchase the carp. No sooner had Shan Ts'ai bought the fish than he took him to the sea and released him.

When the son returned to his father the Dragon King, he told him all that had happened. Deeply moved by this act of compassion, the great king ordered that Miao Shan be presented with a pearl of such luminosity that she would be able to read at night in the glow of its magic light.

When Lung Nu, the daughter of the third son, heard what had happened, she begged permission to take the pearl to Miao Shan and then to stay with her and study the scriptures and devotions of the Buddhist faith. Permission was granted and so Lung Nu came to Miao Shan, who was so taken by Lung Nu's sincerity that she asked her to stay with her and Shan Ts'ai. The two disciples of Miao Shan addressed each other as brother and sister and have remained by her side to this day.

Meanwhile, back in the palace, the king's life went from bad to worse. Cursed by the gods for his bloody usurpation of the throne and by the Buddha for his treatment of Miao Shan, he fell ill with a severe form of jaundice. His whole body was afflicted and broke into sores. He was unable to sleep or rest, tossing and turning by day and night. All the doctors of the kingdom were summoned, but none could halt the spread and development of the disease. In desperation they tried every known cure but to no effect, for this was no ordinary ailment. His two older daughters and their husbands feasted and rejoiced, believing that they would soon inherit the kingdom and caring nothing for the distress of their father the king.

Then, as the king lay at death's door, a strange monk suddenly appeared in the palace, claiming that he could cure him. 'I have a divine remedy that will heal Your Majesty,' he said.

The king asked, 'What medicine do you have with you that can do this?'

The monk said, 'If you take the arm and eye of one who is without anger, combine them into a medicine and apply it, you will be cured.'

The king and his advisers were horrified by this. 'Where could I find such a person willing to make such a sacrifice for one like me?' asked the king.

The monk replied, 'On Hsiang Shan you will find such a person. She is an immortal whose devotion to the Buddhist faith has brought her to the stage of perfection. She has no anger and will respond to your request.'

Immediately the king ordered a messenger to set out for Hsiang Shan to find this wonderful immortal and to beg for the ingredients of this terrible strange prescription. The messenger was saddled and gone within minutes.

But all was not well in the palace. The two sons-in-law heard of the strange monk and feared lest the king recover and they lose their chance to reign. So they plotted together. They determined to poison the king that very night and to kill the monk so that the blame for the king's death could be placed upon his shoulders. They intended to present the king with a broth which they would claim was the medicine prescribed by the monk. This way they would deal with both king and monk.

They were not alone, however. Lurking within the palace was the spirit on duty that day. Hearing this evil plan, he determined to foil them.

Later that evening, the two sons-in-law appeared in the king's bedroom bearing a bowl of poisoned soup.

'This is the medicine the monk has prescribed. Please drink this, Your Majesty, and be returned to full health,' they said.

But before the king could lift it to his lips, the door burst open and in rushed the spirit on duty that day. With a whirlwind he knocked the bowl to the floor and felled the two villains. Bowing before the king, he explained the reason for his actions and the king, aghast at this treachery, had his two sons-in-law bound hand and foot and taken off to prison.

Meanwhile, elsewhere in the palace, the assassin selected by the sons-in-law crept into the room where the monk lay asleep. Raising his sword, he brought it down upon the recumbent figure. But as the blade touched the robes of the monk, it became entangled. As the astonished murderer watched, the robes arose by themselves and wrapped themselves so tightly around the assassin that he could not move. But within the robes there was no body, for the monk had disappeared as mysteriously as he had arrived.

When the failed assassin was found the next day, he was tried and executed along with the two treacherous sons-in-law and it was only the pleas of the queen which saved her two daughters.

While all this was unfolding at the palace, the messenger rode on through the day and night, arriving at Hsiang Shan at dawn. Finding Miao Shan, he knelt before her and delivered his message. She looked down and said, 'My father has shown disrespect for the Three Great Treasures of the Buddhist faith. He has tried to suppress the truth and has murdered innocent nuns. This should bring retribution.'

So saying, she smiled upon the messenger, gouged out her eyes and cut off both arms, which she laid before the astonished and horrified messenger. As her offerings were gathered up, the whole Earth shook at the momentousness of these actions.

Before the messenger left, Miao Shan said, 'Tell the king to turn from his evil ways and to embrace the True Path.'

When the messenger arrived back, he found the monk awaiting him by the palace gate. Handing over the gruesome trophies of his journey, the messenger went directly to the king to report his success. Moments later the monk strode into the king's chamber, to the bewilderment of all, bearing a medical preparation. But without question, the king drank it and instantly he was restored to full health.

Falling on his knees, he offered his thanks to the monk. But the monk dismissed this, saying, 'Why do you thank me? You should be thanking the one who gave her eyes and arms to heal you.' So saying, he suddenly disappeared from their sight, never to be seen again.

The king and queen ordered their carriages to be made ready and with the whole court following, set off that very day for Hsiang Shan.

Arriving before the Bodhisattva, they bowed low and offered their thanks to the mutilated woman who stood before them. As the queen lifted her eyes to gaze upon the one who had saved her husband, she uttered a shriek of horror and astonishment, for she recognized that it was none other than her youngest daughter Miao Shan. The king, realizing what she had done for him, despite all he had done to her, fell prostrate upon the floor and asked her forgiveness.

Miao Shan said, 'I am indeed Miao Shan. Mindful of my father's love, I have repaid him with my eyes and arms.'

Overcome with emotion, her parents embraced her and the king said, 'I am so evil that I have caused my daughter terrible suffering.'

Miao Shan replied, 'Father, I have suffered no pain. Having given up these human eyes, I shall see with diamond eyes. Having yielded up these mortal arms, I shall receive golden arms. If my vow is true, all this will follow.'

At these words, the mountain and indeed the whole world shook. Great clouds of many colours descended, a wonderful fragrance filled the air and divine flowers rained down everywhere. When the clouds lifted, Miao Shan was revealed as the Thousand-Armed and Thousand-Eyed Kuan Yin. Hovering above her parents, she bade them return home and rule justly according to the Buddhist faith. Then the Bodhisattva Kuan Yin, accompanied by Shan Ts'ai and Lung Nu, ascended into the clouds, the Bodhisattva radiating beauty like the harvest moon.

Weeping and also rejoicing at this revelation, the king and queen buried the mortal remains of their daughter and built a beautiful shrine over her body. Then, praising Kuan Yin, they returned to the palace and ruled for many years, teaching love and compassion and drawing the hearts of all in their kingdom into knowledge of the truth of the Buddhist faith.

This extraordinary story is the very heart of the Kuan Yin cultus and in various forms, many far more elaborate and convoluted than this version, is performed, sung, painted, carved, recited and lived throughout China to this day.

Kuan Yin and the Sea

The third type of story is what might best be called a miraculous deliverance story of the sea.

The sacred island of Kuan Yin, Pu To, is set in the sea, 70 miles from Ningbo and on the main trade routes to Korea and Japan. It is therefore hardly surprising that legends are associated with Kuan Yin and the sea. But it is also probably true that many of the typical stories of Kuan Yin's miraculous intervention to save sailors or travellers at sea have been taken over from local sea goddesses. Along the coast of China, there are numerous cults of sea goddesses, often known only in the area of one or two ports or harbours.

For example, the Portuguese colony of Macau takes its name from the corruption of the title of the main temple on the peninsula. This temple (known as a *gau* in Cantonese) is dedicated to the sea goddess A-Ma. Hence in Cantonese it is called the A-Ma *gau* – which has become Macau. A-Ma is worshipped by the fisher folk and her temple is filled with models or carvings of ships, with anchors and with other nautical offerings of grateful sailors. Yet her worship is apparently restricted to just this area, for in

Hong Kong, there is another sea goddess with different stories attached to her. This is repeated up and down the coast of China.

Kuan Yin, however, does have a more vital role in many of the sea or water legends than the average sea goddess. For whereas the sea goddesses save ships but do not basically try to alter the state of affairs, Kuan Yin, in her role as the Compassionate One, does more than just rescue the needy. She works to make life easier and to tame the wilder aspects of the seas and rivers in order to protect people. The following is a typical example of a Kuan Yin and the seas story.

THE BRIDGE OF FUKIEN

The Lo Yang river in Fukien was one of the busiest, broadest and most dangerous rivers in China. Down it came great barges bearing foods and raw materials from the heartland of China. Up it came great ships from countries far away. The wide estuary mouth of the river offered many ways to the main river and the river itself was broad enough to carry this huge trade. However, the river was also dangerous, with fast currents and eddies. Many died in its treacherous waters and every attempt to erect a bridge across its narrowest point failed, with much loss of life.

One morning, without warning, a terrible typhoon swept in from the sea. The river turned into a boiling mass of waves and foam and the ships on it were cast this way and that. The wind ripped up houses on either side and raised waves over 30 feet (9 m) tall.

In the midst of this mayhem, a small passenger boat was caught up. Filled with families and traders, it was cast first this way then that. Waves swept over it, cutting out the very daylight. Children were thrown against the railings, baskets of chickens scattered to the four winds and only by holding on for dear life did the passengers survive. But it was clear that there was no way the ship would make it to the shore. It was only a matter of time before the waves engulfed it and it sank. On board, the passengers cried out for help, praying for deliverance from the storm and the surging waters.

As the boat dipped even more dramatically and it appeared their time had come, the passengers suddenly saw the figure of a tall woman dressed in flowing white robes who appeared on the prow

of the boat. Closing her eyes, she raised her hands before the raging waters, which immediately ceased their turbulence. Turning to face the winds, she opened her eyes and the winds died down and the storm clouds dispersed. Then the woman turned again to face the astonished passengers and they realized that this was none other than Kuan Yin herself. They fell to their knees in devotion. Kuan Yin drifted effortlessly down the becalmed ship until she stood before a pregnant woman who was still clinging to the railing, her face ashen with fear.

Bending down, Kuan Yin touched the woman and said, 'Fong Ts'ai, have no fear, nor offer me any thanks. For you will give birth to a son who will tame this river. He will build a bridge across it.'

So saying, Kuan Yin disappeared.

Not long after Fong Ts'ai gave birth to her son and she named him Ts'ai Hsiang. As he grew up he proved to be a good and obedient son. Every year at the time of the great storm when Kuan Yin had appeared, his mother would remind him of Kuan Yin's promise.

'My son, you must let nothing stand in the way of your building the bridge,' she would say. And the boy would nod solemnly.

Ts'ai Hsiang studied hard and proved to be a brilliant student. He graduated his way up through the ranks of the civil service, being moved from place to place, until he was appointed Prime Minister by the Emperor. Here he proved himself to be both wise and just. Honour after honour was heaped upon him. Yet he was not comfortable. Always at the back of his mind was the bridge story. He had failed to undertake this task and he was beginning to grow old. But whenever he asked permission from the Emperor to return to Fukien, the Emperor would refuse, anxious not lose the advice of his minister for even one day.

One evening, much troubled by all this, Ts'ai Hsiang wandered into the Imperial Garden. There he sat and watched as an army of ants marched past, carrying food to their nest. The sight of the orderly ranks of the ants gave him an idea. Before dawn the next day, he sneaked into the Imperial Gardens. Making sure he was not observed, he wrote eight characters with a broad brush dipped in honey upon the wide leaves of a tree in the garden. This done, he crept out the way he had come.

Later that morning the Emperor went for his usual constitutional around the gardens. All of a sudden he spotted the heaving mass of ants that had been attracted to the honey. He rubbed his eyes in amazement, for the scurrying ants spelt out eight characters, which he read out aloud, saying: 'Ts'ai Hsiang, return home to fulfil your duty.'

At this Ts'ai Hsiang ran into the gardens, kowtowed before the Emperor and said, 'Thank you, thank you, for your permission to return home.'

The Emperor was startled and began to deny that he had given any such order, protesting that he was just reading aloud. But Ts'ai Hsiang interrupted him, saying, 'Every word Your Imperial

Majesty utters is a divinely inspired command. I quake and obey!'

At this the Emperor, not wishing to look foolish, gave his permission, but told Ts'ai Hsiang that he could only be gone for two months.

No sooner did Ts'ai Hsiang reach home than he began work on the bridge. Vast gangs of labourers were hired and wagons filled with stone rumbled down to the chosen place on the banks of the mighty river. However, the river was so strong that even the most massive stones were as sand in the water and no foundation could successfully be laid.

As the days turned into weeks, Ts'ai Hsiang became desperate, for the time for him to return to the Imperial Court was drawing inexorably nearer. So he decided to address an appeal to the Sea Dragon King, asking him to hold back the waters for three days to enable the foundations to be laid.

Once the letter had been composed and sealed with his Imperial seal, Ts'ai Hsiang went to speak to his workmen, asking for a volunteer to go down into the sea and deliver the message to the Sea Dragon King. Needless to say, no one was very keen. Then, as the request was spoken again, a not very bright workman called Hsia Te Hai misheard what was being said and, thinking someone was needed to run a message to the local prefect, he volunteered. Too late did he discover what the nature of his errand really was!

Escorted by the soldiers of Ts'ai Hsiang's personal guard, the unfortunate workman was brought to the edge of the sea at nightfall, clutching the letter in his hand. Here he was abandoned to await the coming of the Sea Dragon King or to venture into the ocean to find him.

Worn out by fear and anxiety, Hsia fell into a fitful sleep. In his sleep he dreamed that he was indeed standing in the Great Hall under the Ocean of the Sea Dragon King. Seeing the Sea Dragon King on his bejewelled throne, Hsia ran forward and kowtowed before him.

'My Lord, I, I, I am Hsia . . . Hsia . . . I am a workman and I bring you this . . . this . . . letter from the Prime . . . Prime . . . Minister,' he stammered in abject terror.

The Sea Dragon King had the letter brought to him and he read it carefully and thoughtfully. Then he turned to the trembling Hsia and said, 'I have read the Prime Minister's request. I shall do as he says. But mark my words. Only three days shall I hold back the waters. On the fourth day they will return, come what may. I mark your hand with these characters to signify my assent. Now be gone.'

Hsia stirred. He stretched. He found that it was sunrise and he was lying on the damp sands by the sea. Looking at his hand he saw strange characters painted upon it. Without any more ado, he ran to the house of the Prime Minister. Forcing his way past the guards, he burst in upon the slumbering minister.

'Sir, Sir, I have seen the Sea Dragon King. Look, he gave me this message for you.'

So saying, he laid his hand with the characters inscribed upon it upon the quilt of Ts'ai Hsiang's bed. Ts'ai Hsiang read, 'The twenty-first day at the Yu hour.'

On the twenty-first day at the Yu hour – five in the afternoon – a vast crowd gathered to see what would happen. At six exactly, the great waters were rolled and sucked back to reveal the rock bed below. Immediately, 1,000 workmen poured down onto the river bed and began to construct the foundation pillars. Ts'ai Hsiang made offerings of incense to the Sea Dragon King and began to order the deployment of his workers.

They toiled all night and into the next day, but despite their greatest efforts, by the end of the first 24 hours, they were less than a quarter of the way through building the bridge. Ts'ai Hsiang realized that he could ask no more than they were already giving from his workers. What he needed was three times the number of workers. But his money, great as it was, would not stretch to this. In despair he saw that with what he had, the bridge would never be finished before the waters rushed back at the end of the third day. He felt as if he was bound to fail and his thoughts went back to his mother and her words. The thought of how the goddess Kuan Yin had saved his mother's life gave him an idea. Kneeling down and making offerings, he called upon the goddess.

'Kuan Yin, you who saved the life of my mother, you who gave me this task, hear my prayers, Most Compassionate One. I have no more money to complete this task. Hear the prayers of your servant and come to my aid. Goddess of Mercy, help me.'

No sooner had he finished praying than a boat appeared as if from nowhere. Standing in the prow of the boat was a tall woman dressed in flowing white robes. Her beauty was of such magnificence even the sun was eclipsed by it. Her loveliness was as the pale moon and her gentleness shone from her face. All who saw her were moved by such a wonderful woman and word soon spread, bringing people from all the surrounding areas to the river bank. Slowly, slowly the boat drifted down the river until it drew close to the bank where the people had gathered.

Now seated in the boat, the woman addressed the crowd. When she spoke, it was as if the leaves of the trees murmured and streams of clear water ran over pebbles. Every man's heart was captivated.

She said, 'I promise to marry whichever man can throw a piece of gold or silver into my lap.'

No sooner were these words spoken than showers of gold coins, silver coins, ornaments, rings and such like descended upon her. But no matter how hard people tried, not a single piece landed in her lap, but fell instead onto the broad cloak which surrounded her.

Soon the boat was so full of gold and silver that it looked as if it would sink, so she held up her hand and forbade any further offerings. Then she summoned Ts'ai Hsiang to approach the boat. Fearfully he came forward.

'Ts'ai Hsiang,' she said, 'I heard your prayers and I have come to help you as you requested. Take all this money, all this gold and silver and use it to complete the bridge. Thus will my prophecy be fulfilled.'

Ts'ai Hsiang's mouth fell open as he realized that here before him stood the goddess Kuan Yin herself. Then with a smile, she disappeared in a wisp of smoke.

Ts'ai Hsiang ordered the gold and silver counted. As soon as he knew how much he had, he sent out orders for 5,000 more workmen. By the end of the second day he had assembled a great force. Promising them double their normal wages if they finished in time, he set them to work.

All the men worked without ceasing. Stone after stone was heaved into position and layer after layer of the bridge began to spread out across the river bed. The great bridge was completed one hour before the mighty waters were released again. The bridge of Kuan Yin had been built, just as she had prophesied.

The Miracles of Kuan Yin

It is worth at this stage taking a closer look at how Kuan Yin acts in and through compassion.

Kuan Yin is not a magician. She can only work with what is, even if she can then produce the most amazing results. The miracles of Kuan Yin are not tricks or feats that she works upon people regardless of who they are. Rather, in the true sense of the Chinese understanding of fate, she works with what is.

In classical Chinese thought, fate determines certain aspects of your life. For example, whether you will be born into a wealthy family or a poor one; what sex you are; whether you will be born healthy or weak. These things are fixed and in many cases are the results of your previous lives and thus the consequence of reincarnation. So, if you are born with, say, a withered arm, that shows you were bad in your previous life and this time round you have to wear off the bad karma you built up. If you do so, then you will be born without any serious physical defect in your next life on Earth.

But beyond these few things, you are in charge of your own fate and destiny. You can change your fortune. This often confuses those whose grasp of Chinese notions of fate is dictated by popular Chinese horoscopes. But even at the most popular level, the Chinese view such things as their 'personality' as, say, a Snake, as being indicators of likely trends rather than as hard and fast regulations of what you are and can do. There is always the possibility – for good or for bad – of change. For example, an act of kindness by someone not renowned for such acts can change their fortune.

The story is told of an old Taoist monk who was a master in physiognomy – reading the face and body. He had a young servant boy who was about eight years old. One day the monk looked at the boy's face and saw there that he would die within the next few months. Saddened by this, he told the boy to take a long holiday and go and visit his parents. 'Take your time,' said the monk. 'Don't hurry back.' For he felt the boy should be with his family when he died.

Three months later, to his astonishment, the monk saw the boy walking back up the mountain. When he arrived he looked intently at his face and saw that the boy would now live to a ripe old age.

'Tell me everything that happened while you were away,' said the monk.

So the boy started to tell of his journey down from the mountain. He told of villages and towns he passed through, of rivers forded and mountains climbed. Then he told how one day he came upon a stream in flood. He noticed, as he tried to pick his way across the flowing stream, that a colony of ants had become trapped on a small island formed by the flooding stream. Moved by compassion for these poor creatures, he took a branch of a tree and laid it across one flow of the stream until it touched the little island. As the ants made their way across, the boy held the branch steady, until he was sure all the ants had escaped to dry land. Then he went on his way.

'So,' thought the old monk to himself, 'that is why the gods have lengthened his days.'

Compassionate acts can alter your fate. Conversely, acts of viciousness can adversely affect your fate.

It is in this context that the miracle stories of Kuan Yin need to be understood. She can offer a fresh start, but does not wipe out the past. She works with what is already there or with the potential for change. The story of the bridge, above, is a good example of this. But there are also more modern examples.

THE HEALING OF CHAO YING

A Chinese colleague of mine, a very brilliant lawyer, has his own tale to tell of Kuan Yin. Let us call him Chao Ying, as he does not wish to be named.

Chao Ying was very successful and quite wealthy. He was also a good Kung Fu master and took great pride in his physical fitness and in his agility, both mental and physical. He also loved fast cars and, to be honest, reckless driving.

One day, somewhat high after a success in the lawcourts in Manchester, UK, he went for a drive and crashed. The crash was a horrific one in which two other people died as a result of his driving. Chao Ying himself was left totally paralysed from the neck downwards. He could not speak or move. All he could do was hear and move his eyes. His entire life was shattered.

For three months he lay in the hospital, unable to move, being fed by nurses and unable to do anything. He thought he would go mad.

He had been brought up in a devout Buddhist family but with success of the material kind and with his own confidence in his physical and mental skills, he had ignored Buddhism for years. Now he found himself thinking again of the core teachings and in particular of Kuan Yin, the Goddess of Compassion. He began to pray that she would help him in some way. He also acknowledged the foolishness of the path he had been on.

One night he awoke. A strange light filled the ward, but no one else seemed to be troubled by it. Then he saw a tall woman in white drift through the main window at the far end of the ward. Effortlessly she glided down the rows of beds until she came to his. By now he was full of both fear and astonishment. The beautiful woman turned towards him and he saw that she was none other than Kuan Yin. Gently she touched his face, his neck, his arms and hands, his chest and his waist. Then she disappeared.

In his grief at her disappearance, he lifted his arms to reach out to her. Then he realized what he had just done. Movement had returned to his arms and hands, to his face and to his body from the waist upwards. But he was still paralysed from the waist downwards.

Chao Ying is still in a wheelchair, but he writes and works as much as he can. His understanding is that Kuan Yin answered his prayers, but that she could not restore him to full health because of the deaths he had caused and because he had been at fault in the arrogance of his attitudes and the foolishness of his actions prior to the accident. She was able to restore him to a certain degree, but not completely.

MONKEY

Perhaps one of the finest examples of the way Kuan Yin works is the Monkey story. This is one of the most popular novels in China and was written in the late sixteenth century. It takes an historical incident – the pilgrimage of Hsuan Tsang (c. AD 596–664) – and weaves around it the most wonderful set of stories and tales concerning the help he has en route from three very disreputable characters, Monkey, Pigsy and Sandy. Their adventures are told in the novel *Journey to the West*. If you have never read this wonderful book, do so! It is a classic of religious humour and adventure and I strongly recommend the abridged version by Arthur Waley, published as *Monkey* (Mandala, 1989).[3]

I cannot give you a full account of the story here for it is long and complex. But I want to look at what happens to the three key dynamic characters, Monkey, Pigsy and Sandy.

The book opens with a series of adventures in which Monkey, King of the Monkeys on Earth, gradually acquires more and more magical powers and comes close to overthrowing the very courts of Heaven. Interestingly enough, he defeats Lao Tzu, foils the

Queen Mother of the West and out-fights the Marshals of the Heavenly Armies. In the end, it takes the Buddha, assisted by Kuan Yin, to capture him. For his crimes he is buried alive under a vast mountain and kept in check by powerful charms inscribed upon the mountain face.

One day, 500 years after Monkey has thus been trapped, Kuan Yin comes before the Buddha in Heaven and asks permission to go to China and find a monk. This monk, she explains, will then travel to India in order to find the life-giving scriptures which, once brought back to China, will lead millions to release from suffering. The description of Kuan Yin is a lovely example of how the goddess was viewed by the sixteenth century:

> Her knowledge fills out the four virtues,
> Her wisdom suffuses her golden body.
> Her necklace is hung with pearls and precious jade,
> Her bracelet is composed of jewels.
> Her hair is like dark clouds wondrously coiffured like
>   curling dragons;
> Her embroidered girdle sways like a phoenix's wing in
>   flight.
> Sea-green jade buttons,
> A gown of pure silk,
> Awash with Heavenly light;
> Eyebrows as if crescent moons,
> Eyes like stars.
> A radiant jade face of divine joyfulness,
> Scarlet lips, a splash of colour.
> Her bottle of Heavenly dew overflows,
> Her willow twig rises from it in full flower.
> She delivers from all the eight terrors,
> Saves all living beings,
> For boundless is her compassion.
> She resides on T'ai Shan,
> She dwells in the Southern Ocean.
> She saves all the suffering when their cries reach her,
> She never fails to answer their prayers,
> Eternally divine and wonderful.[4]

The Buddha agrees to her request for permission to undertake this search for a monk who will bring the scriptures of the Mahayana, Great Vehicle School of Buddhism, to China. To assist her chosen disciple, the Buddha tells her: 'As you journey to China to find your monk, if you encounter any devils with great magical powers, you should persuade them to reform and become disciples of the pilgrim who will come to find the scriptures.'

He then gives her three headbands which should be placed on such devils so that if their wicked nature tries to reassert itself when they are accompanying the pilgrim monk, he can cause them to suffer such a dreadful headache that they will learn to obey.

Off goes Kuan Yin and sure enough, she does meet such characters on her journey – Monkey, Pigsy and Sandy. Each of them is guilty of some terrible crime which has either led to punishment, such as Monkey being buried under the mountain for 500 years, or they have become outcasts, eating human beings or terrorizing a neighbourhood.

Pigsy and Sandy both leap out to attack Kuan Yin and her servant Moksa, only to find that their powers are to no avail against the goddess who, for instance, quells Pigsy by casting a lotus flower before him in the midst of a ferocious battle with Moksa. She then offers them the chance of reform and salvation from their past deeds if they will accompany the pilgrim she will send on his journey to India. Each gratefully agrees and awaits the coming of the pilgrim.

When the pilgrim passes by on his way to India, the three duly join up and begin on the path to reform. But their journey to India and to reform is not an easy one. The monk, Tripitaka, has to use the magic headband to control them, and Monkey and Pigsy in particular try everything in their power to avoid being reformed! Time and time again it is only the intervention of Kuan Yin that puts the pilgrim band together again and it is only she who can remind them of their higher purpose. But even she sometimes has a hard time of it!

Eventually of course, they are reformed and the scriptures are brought to China. But the story captures perfectly the interaction between Kuan Yin's compassion and the personalities with which she has to contend. The salvation of the three evil-doers is a joint and collaborative venture with the goddess or in this case the

Bodhisattva Kuan Yin. She cannot overcome their innate natures. They themselves have to do this, in collaboration with her, even if at times they have to be cajoled into doing it.

It is a wonderful story and captures exactly how Kuan Yin works. Miracles are within her provenance but her real powers lie in transforming through the individual, taking what is inherent and bringing the best out of everyone. Perhaps the heart of the appeal of Kuan Yin is at one level that she does not take you over, but works with and through you. She is both the Goddess of Compassion and our companion, on our journeys through life and beyond.

Endnotes

1. Glen Dudbridge, *The Legend of Miao-shan*, Ithica Press for the Board of the Faculty of Oriental Studies, Oxford, 1978, to which I am much indebted.
2. Op. cit., page 17.
3. Wu Ch'eng-en, *Monkey*, trans. Arthur Waley, Mandala, 1989.
4. Adapted from W. J. F. Jenner, trans., *Journey to the West*, Foreign Language Press, Beijing, 1982, Chapter 8, pp. 135–6.

3

THE POEMS OF
KUAN YIN

INTRODUCTION

Martin Palmer

The third part of our book contains 100 poems which for centuries have been associated with Kuan Yin. I have found versions of these poems being used in the crowded temples of Hong Kong such as Wong Tai Sin; I have discussed them high on Taoist Sacred Mountains in China, such as Hua Shan; I have seen them being read in tiny, humble shrines in the countryside of China and in the great temples of Beijing; I have found them to hand in the homes of Chinese friends in the UK and Canada. For they have spread around the Chinese world and are as ubiquitous as the goddess herself. But what exactly are they? What is their power or mystery? Where do they come from? And how are they used?

How Are They Used?

As with all Chinese texts associated with divination, the poems can be used in two different ways.

First, they can be turned to by simply opening the book at random and allowing the poem that your eye lights upon to speak to you in whatever way is appropriate – perhaps as meditation, perhaps as revelation, perhaps as challenge or even as correction.

The second method is the one you can observe in just about every temple or monastery in the Chinese world. This involves the use of 100 small, thin wooden sticks.

Let us imagine that you wish to ask the goddess for advice about your job or about your family affairs. Arriving at the temple, you would buy paper money and joss sticks to offer to your ancestors and to the gods by burning them in the great urns erected at the entrance to each temple for this purpose. Having made your obeisance and offerings, you then take a pot filled with 100 numbered sticks, each stick having a number from 1 to 100. Having prepared your mind by clearing it of unworthy thoughts, you kneel before the main temple or in front of an image of Kuan Yin and murmur your request for advice. Then, still kneeling, you tilt the pot or container, all the while shaking it until the sticks begin to move up and out of the pot. The art is to shake it in such a way that gradually a few sticks rise higher than the rest and begin to teeter on the edge. Eventually one of these will fall out – sometimes more, in which case you can refer to all the numbers given.

The stick which has fallen out has a number on it – let us assume for the sake of argument that it is 56. You then have two courses open to you. You can either refer to your own copy of the *Poems*, which you can buy in some of the major temples compounds and thus find out what no. 56 has to say to your specific request, or you can go to the fortune-teller. Seated in booths around the temple – not so frequently in mainland China, but you can find them if you know who to ask and where to go – are fortune-tellers who will give you the reading.

Let me use no. 56 as an example:

> The stream bubbles and sings over its bed of pebbles,
> The wind is keen, the moon bright, the high ones are glad –
> And after asking about the path of all your striving, see this:
> The scent of the forest flowers comes from the right conditions.

It is very unlikely that you would be given a reading of the poem which would do what Jay has done – bring out the poetic beauty and imagery within. For each poem can be read at three different levels at least. First there is the poetic level, which contains insights, images and visions which are in themselves revelatory. This is what we have provided.

The second level is to read the poem at an allegorical level but through fairly rigid divinational glasses. Thus no. 56 is traditionally described as meaning:

Someone works very hard,
But nothing is achieved, even if he tries his hardest.
Therefore it is best to wait and see what happens.
In the end all will be well.

The poetry has gone, along with the imagery, but the text is now well on its way to transformation into a divination text suited to the usual, rather mundane questions which those seeking fortune-teller's advice wish to have answered.

The third level is the interpretation of what this re-interpreted poem means according to 14 basic areas of concern, which are: the family; business; finances; marriage; pregnancy; visitors; animal husbandry; farming; lost relatives or friends; legal cases; moving house; finding that which is lost; illness; ancestors.

Thus in answer to the questions about business or family affairs, no. 56 would give readings which assure you that your business will do well and you will have a prosperous year and that your marriage is on firm foundations and you can expect a baby boy soon.

We have moved quite a way from the poem!

When we were working on this translation, our colleague Man-Ho Kwok was very hesitant about how we should interpret the poems. Sometimes we found ourselves arguing quite strongly about the interpretation. While I wished to explore the imagery of the poems, drawing as they did upon some of the most significant images and metaphors in Chinese culture, Man-Ho was keen to look at them in terms of the traditional divinational understanding of the poems, which almost completely ignores the poetic imagery. We had a number of spirited discussions about this!

In the end, we opted for the poetic imagery for reasons which will be spelt out further on in this introduction and in Jay's piece on his experience of putting them back into poetry.

What is important to stress here is that for those who use the poems in a full traditional divinational way, these poems are divine revelations from the goddess herself – revealed texts on a par with the Qur'an or the Bible. In taking the approach that we have, we are not denying the inspirational dimension of the poems. Far from it. But we are looking at how the inspiration of Kuan Yin spoke to and through the writings of various poets who sought through their poetry to express something of the divine feminine in wisdom.

Who Uses Them?

On the whole these poems are consulted, as are all such 100-text divination books, by women. As with so many faiths, it is the women who tend the temples and their deities, and who look after all the details of cleaning and caring for the statues. It is also the women who express greatest concern for the issues which such divination focuses upon – family health, well-being, marriage, children and so forth. Men will come when financial troubles loom or when exams have to be done. Otherwise it is the women who come to ask help from the goddess.

The Kuan Yin poems are just one amongst a considerable array of divination books containing poems, usually ascribed to a major deity. Some are simply called Heavenly Divination Stick Predictions. Others are associated with deities such as Kuan Di, the god of war, the Jade Emperor, ruler of the Taoist Heaven, or a local deity like Wong Tai Sin in Hong Kong. They all fulfil the same basic purpose: to provide divinatory oracular insights and guidance. As such they are the continuation of a line which began with the development of the *I Ching*.

The *I Ching* began as oracle readings given by divination using oracle bones of tortoise shell or ox bone. Each of the oracles at the start of each hexagram is an actual reading given over a relatively short period of a year or so in the eleventh century BC. These oracles led to and guided the successful uprising of the Chou tribes against the corrupt and oppressive Shang dynasty. Each year they were recited at the Chou ancestral temple in an annual re-enactment of the rebellion against the Shang and the establishment of the Chou dynasty. They were originally given under the guidance of the shamans, but the shamans began to lose power and authority, as I have described earlier, and as the oracles were used annually, they began to be used as written texts of guidance. The notion of seeking a new oracle each time a question had to be asked began to be seen as old-fashioned, costly and time-consuming. The *I Ching* marks the shift from a shaman based, oracular culture to one which used and reused earlier oracles as guidance.[1]

In consulting the *I Ching* in its earliest days, yarrow sticks were used and it is from these that the 100 divination sticks of today descend.

Each temple will have a number of such divination books, each containing 100 poems or sayings. Amongst these the Kuan Yin book is one of the most common and most frequently consulted. The style of these divination books varies. Some contain sayings or oracles which are short and pithy – say just two lines of five characters. Others have the four-line sequence of the Kuan Yin poems, but may have only five characters per poem. In each case it is obvious that an array of material has been gradually collated and compiled to fit a prescribed pattern and then produced under one overarching title. These collections first appear in the thirteenth century and have changed little in style and format from that time.

What Are the Kuan Yin Poems?

Our contention is that the Kuan Yin poems are a collection made in the fifteenth to sixteenth centuries, possibly using older material dating from the twelfth to fifteenth centuries. The poems all fit the same format, four lines of seven characters each. The use of a set style and pattern for a collection of poems is typically Chinese. Competitions would often be held in which poets, or those with poetic aspirations, would be given a style and format and subject and expected to produce a poem immediately. The ability to do so was highly prized by the literati of China.

In Imperial China, the poet was greatly honoured and prized. Many scholars and officials would try their own hand at versification. A temple dedicated to Kuan Yin would have drawn many poets, and aspiring poets would quite easily have found patrons and sponsors in as affluent a place as Hangchow. Inspired by both the beauty of the site and the femininity and divinity of Kuan Yin, poets would produce poems which would be offered to the temple. Probably some were carved upon stone steles and erected within the grounds of the temple. Others would have become well known and would have been recited by literary visitors. Yet others would have been written down, mounted upon scrolls and displayed in the visitors' quarters of the temple and monastery. In other words, poems and temples went together in a way which is difficult for non-Chinese to appreciate.

The poems themselves in the Kuan Yin collection vary considerably. Some are superb pieces of poetic writing, full of imagery and literary allusions. Some are profoundly moving for their simplicity and beauty. But some are rather pedestrian, showing the variety of poets whose works are collected here. Like any anthology, they contain the magnificent, the good and the average. In fact the idea of an anthology is not a bad one to use when trying to understand this book.

But who compiled it, where and when and why?

We have tried to look at internal evidence and at external data which could help us give some idea of the provenance and date of these poems. Our conclusions are that they reflect a wealthy, even a retired society of scholar administrators, the sort of men who had risen high in the bureaucracy of Imperial China and had thus made their money and then retired to some beauty spot where they could live a life of simple comfort, devoting themselves to religion, philosophy, poetry and good dinners.

Just such a place, prized for its natural beauty, was, and to some extent still is, Hangchow. Here you will recall, was the major centre of Kuan Yin devotion throughout the period from about 1200 to 1400, when Pu To overtook it. But it continued to be a major centre until very recently.

What could be more natural than that the retired scholarly, bureaucratic society of Hangchow should chose the most famous and beautiful deity in China, whose centre was in their town, as a subject for poems? This is what we believe happened.

The style of the poems points us towards the settled time of the Ming dynasty (AD 1368–1644), thus the fourteenth to sixteenth centuries. The picture which comes across is of a contented world where no major threats disturb the peace and where honesty will bring its rewards. This seems to us to indicate the society at Hangchow.

But why was this book produced and for what purpose?

This is almost impossible to answer, so what follows is conjecture. In a city as famous as Hangchow, there were many tourists from as early as the tenth century. The Chinese have always loved to explore and visit their own country. Gazetteers of the most famous places such as the Sacred Mountains or famous cities such as Hangchow go back to the twelfth and thirteenth centuries. Often such books would contain famous poems written by the great and not so great poets of China on visiting a site. This is what we believe lies behind this book.

The temple of Shang Tien Chu in Hangchow was the most famous land-based shrine of Kuan Yin. To it came literally hundreds of thousands of pilgrims every year. A good many of them would have been men of letters. Their ideal souvenir would have been some poems about Kuan Yin or inspired by her, for Chinese poetry likes to use a given starting-point in order to launch off into a host of themes and images. These poems, bought as a souvenir, would be taken home to be read at leisure. Our contention is that the Kuan Yin divination poems originally began life in just such a way.

Whether they were also designed to be used as divination texts is hard to tell, but it seems highly likely that they would have been soon used in such a way within a very short period of time.

The other possibility is that the temple authorities wanted to try and outdo the emerging centre on Pu To Shan. By producing their own divination texts they could have captured a certain section of the tourist/pilgrim market. The raw materials for such a book lay around them in the poems written about or inspired by the shrine. It is interesting to note that few of them refer to themselves as oracles or divination texts. The majority are simply poems.

Our belief that Hangchow was the place from which the Kuan Yin poems emerged is strengthened by the remarkable parallels with another, even more famous text, also written in Hangchow. This has become a fundamental religious text, although it was originally written as a humorous novel!

Sometime in the 1570s, the author Wu Cheng'en (1500–82) wrote 100-chapter book called *Journey to the West*. This described the journey which did in fact take place of the monk Hsuan Tsang (*c.* AD 596–664) to India to fetch the scriptures. Wu Cheng'en took this basic plot and added to it the wonderful stories of the Monkey King, Great Sage Equal to Heaven, Pigsy, Sandy and a host of other minor characters. I have given a brief description of this story at the end of Part Two *(see pages 89–93)*.

The book was written as a part humorous, part popular Buddhism novel. It was never intended to be taken as describing actual beings – Monkey *et al* were popular folk figures, developed by Wu's imagination. And the book was written in Hangchow, for the literary, Buddhist scholarly class who resided there and patronized such works.

Today, visit any major Buddhist temple, or even go into Taoist temples in certain places, and you will find pictures, carvings and statues of Monkey and Pigsy being worshipped, along with the pilgrim who is called Tripitaka in the novel. For the wonderful characters invented for the novel have now passed into the pantheon of gods of popular Chinese belief and are inseparable from the true historical figure of the pilgrim monk.

That such a work should arise in Hangchow but should then be developed in such a way offers remarkable parallels which embolden us in our assertion that a very similar process happened to the Kuan Yin poems – and in the same place.

Whatever the truth of their origin, the poems have become part and parcel of the Chinese religious scene. But in doing so, their poetic origins have become obscured and indeed even lost. As far as we know, only one other English translation exists. This was produced in Hong Kong in the early 1980s by the Tung Wah Group. Glancing through the English translation, you would never guess that in the original Chinese, many of these poems are elegant, graceful poetic works. For what has happened is that the translation has on the whole gone for the interpretive understanding of the poems, the fortune-telling dimension, and has lost the poetic.

As I mentioned earlier, we had some vigorous debates about how to translate these poems. In the end we decided to let them speak as poems. It is significant that they have become associated with the goddess; that they have guided people's lives for some 500 to 600 years. However, we believe having studied them in some detail, that the poems themselves are capable of speaking to us in their own ways.

The inspiration for all these poems was and is the Goddess of Mercy, the Compassionate Bodhisattva, the One who Hears the Cries of the World. Over the centuries many have heard her and she has been heard by many. She has touched and shaped lives, offered new hope and brought out the potential within those who felt lost or helpless, or simply overwhelmed. We believe that through the poems of Kuan Yin, the same succour, the same compassion, the same reflection upon our own states of mind and being can be offered to an audience who has never met her before.

The divine feminine cannot be suppressed for long. In China it emerged by the transformation of the male into the female. In our own generation, the rediscovery of the feminine divine has liberated and challenged many. In her own quiet, compassionate way, the voice of Kuan Yin which can be heard in these poems offer us a way of hearing the divine feminine anew. She offers us the hand of compassion and the friendship of the companion, for she is indeed the One who Hears the Cries of the World.

Endnotes

1. See our translation and introduction to the *I Ching*, Palmer, Ramsay, with Zhao, Aquarian, 1995.

INTRODUCTION

Jay Ramsay

The world of the Kuan Yin poems is very different from what we have seen in the *Tao Te Ching* and the *I Ching* – and this is true both formally and in terms of content or substance, though there are similarities too. Mainly the difference comes from the fact that these poems were written very much later in time: they come *after* the great T'ang period of Li Po and Tu Fu, among others, and they are written in an eloquent, compact, gem-like style that had become established as literary Chinese. Their beauty, appropriately enough, is immediately obvious.

The root of Kuan Yin's full name (as Man-Ho pointed out to me, sketching the characters in rough in front of me) means 'look, world, sound' – and these poems are, in every sense, more worldly, as the product of a sophisticated city culture. They are both more aesthetic and more refined: they have a juicy wisdom, a ripeness born out of experience that distinguishes them from the raw shamanic intensity of the *I Ching*, and – in some ways – from the more overtly moralistic agenda of the *Tao Te Ching*, as their language testifies.

But they are not just beautiful poems and it is important to realize this. They are Kuan Yin's – written because of her, under the auspices of her, and at moments as if directly from her, in her voice.

So we have a paradox here: the poems are, on the one hand, more secular – and on the other they are more overtly Divine. To resolve this, we need to understand something about the function of beauty in them, which I believe lies at the heart of what they are and what they can give us now.

A sense of beauty is basic to an emphasis that values feeling – and which affirms that there are things, in the highest and realest sense, that we can only understand through it. If this is an attitude we need to regain now, in a culture short-changed by ugliness, then it is one that is also ancient. We find it in Egypt, we find it in Plato and it lies at the essence of Kuan Yin: in what she does and the way she does it, as all the stories tell. We can't understand the feminine without it either: or the pain that women feel in its absence. And it is not just cosmetic either: we need to understand beauty as a deep thing both on a level of being (an individual, an object or thing), and on a level of response (with feeling, with awareness). And this attitude, fundamentally, is poetry: it is what poetry embodies and represents.

So, turning to our text again, what we have here in these 100 quatrains, freed – as Martin has said – from a level of crude 'this-means-that' interpretation, is an invitation to see wisdom through the eyes of beauty and through the beauty of the natural created order. We are being invited, in other words, to see Spirit *in* Nature, reflected and embodied there – just as She (Kuan Yin) is, in her presence: or in Chinese terms, Heaven *in* Earth, as no. 51 explicitly states:

Yes, Heaven and Earth affect the human mind . . .

and which no. 42, before it, also directly gestures. And the quality of this beauty, the point of it all, which makes these poems 'not just beautiful', is that *it is true*: it is truth. Or try to imagine what truth would be like *without* beauty – and that might be another way of arriving at the essence of what is being presented here and offered through poetry.

There is a hexagram, too, from the *I Ching* that lies behind all of this, that is useful to reflect on – and that is no. 22, 'Adorn', in our translation. These poems are adornments: inspired, written, and subsequently gathered and edited, like cowrie shells on dried grass thread – or like the gem stones of a necklace. And, closer to us in time, in their rich and impacted imagery and their visual quality, they are in many ways like Tarot cards, an analogy I'll be returning to.

I want to say a little now about how they work as poems, before going on to look at how I've handled working with them in terms of translation.

The poems don't follow a linear structure or logical line of argument – they work instead laterally, 'across', by association and juxtaposition (as the *Tao Te Ching* does): in fact so much so, that initially the four lines that make up each poem in the original Chinese can seem unrelated: they appear to make different statements and an absence of conjunctions like 'and' or 'but' reinforces this. We have to infer these. The poems themselves are made up of a combination of image and direct statement: and in their syllabic regularity of four lines of seven characters each (as Martin has noted), they function with an immediacy that is like a haiku or a *koan*. They make the point, and then they leave it there. As poems they are closest in their impact to haiku: and in the best of them, the image is always central, conveying this quality of beauty through the imagination to our own imaginations as we read and reflect on them. In this, and in their taut economy, they prefigure the Imagist movement in poetry in the 1920s, in England and America, which Chinese Poetry was a major inspiration for. The whole idea of Imagism was to let the image speak as the poem, so in Pound's famous 'In a Station of the Metro', you can see how this effect is achieved:

> The apparition of these faces in the crowd:
> Petals on a wet, black bough.

You can see the connection, too, three or four centuries later.

The voice and tone, like the world of these poems, is different too – they are calmer and more detached as creations of a more settled society, and they are also lighter, capable of both irony and humour as well as moments of memorable lightning-like directness. They are serious and they are playful, too. I want to say they are more feminine: and in fact there is no evidence that these were not also written by women. They have all the range of feminine perception and intelligence, with its mercurial shifts of mood and tempo, as well as the compassion, the mercy that is Kuan Yin's alone. They are also, like the *I Ching*, preoccupied with guidance: addressing 100 different archetypal human situations through the figure of the *chun* or wise one following on from the shaman and the sage.

Another thing that became obvious to me as I worked on these is their sequencing and arrangement – and once again, as with the *Tao* and the *I Ching*, there is clearly a deliberate pattern that unfolds a world here, like a fan, or like a peacock spreading its tail feathers. Despite the brevity of these poems, there is a world in them and they offer a world to us.

The cycle begins with a poem about devotion that links to the last poem (no. 100) as a reminder of that: and we then move into a series about real life situations of difficulty which are then spiritualized (nos 8, 9, 10 for instance) before the more specific theme of the emergence of joy and detachment comes in (nos 16 and 19), which in turn leads to the philosophy of these poems alongside the three of them that are specifically in Kuan Yin's voice (nos 30, 36 and 53). A series of positive states of being and response are contrasted with their opposites, in a typically Chinese way (no. 41 for instance); and these in turn give way to a series of meditations on the Self, on who we really are, *and* what separates us from that (nos 58 and 60). From here, the poems go on to evoke a particular emphasis on Spirit in Nature which is central to their vision (no. 69), reaching a peak of awareness around no. 85 before a slow descent leads into how we need to live (no. 91) and again, how *not* to (nos 94 and 99). The entire sequence is held, as in the *I Ching*, by pairing and contrast – positive and negative – so that the effect is of something strung like a T'ang lute, resonating as it's plucked. It is music.

So what is the world-view or vision that these poems offer? In brief, at every turn, we can say that there is an assertion of the Divine that is immanent, in every situation, and in Nature functioning as natural law – just as Kuan Yin herself is present, and uniquely personal in her presence, while at the same time being transcendent and yet never – like the Mother – beyond reach. These poems are correspondingly more personal too than what we have in either the *Tao* or the *I Ching*: they have an intimate, one-to-one quality in speaking to each one of us. Everywhere, too, there is an assertion of *Te* or Virtue, in terms of right thought and right action, and the consequences of that – but again, this isn't offered as something moralistic, but as something natural and inevitable, as inevitable as the consequences of its absence, as no. 60 so strikingly states. And again, everywhere there is a more subtle assertion of the feminine, the yin, in the processes of Nature, so that everywhere the perception of beauty, and beauty as truth, is grounded in the natural world, as it is, as the moon waxes and wanes, and the seasons flourish and decay. Within this, the *Kuan Yin* is a world of metamorphoses, of sophisticated awareness that takes change for granted, and that sees beyond itself into the fabric of its own source that is Heaven: and the mediation of all of this, beyond each individual poet involved here, is the *chun*, the wise one or wise person, the guide who has experienced the world and the way of all things. All of these meanings are in the word *chun*: and the radical meaning of the word (as we discovered) is composed of 'mouth' and 'to direct', suggesting someone who has the authority to speak, counsel or teach. So the *chun* is a teacher too, in its most exalted form – after Kuan Yin – as the Buddha himself (in No, 62), and otherwise as a number of unnamed men or women who are in the service of truth. The constant references to this wise person make the poems almost read like an advertisement for wisdom and an appeal to seek guidance which they also encapsulate, as we read them now.

What I've tried to do with them is a classical first rendition, evoking as much of the tone and feeling of the original as possible. Working within the stricture of the quatrain format has not been easy, because for every Chinese character one needs so many more English words. I realized immediately that these versions could not be regular: so what I've done is deliberately loosen them so that the feeling of each poem can be there, and the sense of it can breathe. I have echoed the tight form of the original instead in natural internal rhyme as it's arisen, as well as in the rhythm of the lines taken together as a whole. I have retained specific references, for instance to the Great Wall in no. 7 and the Emperor in no. 13 – at the same time, I have taken occasional liberties with metaphor that link the sense more directly to our time, in so far as these poems reach – like Kuan Yin herself – beyond a particular time and place, and are global as their world touches ours. I have also, as I did in the *Tao Te Ching*, tried to balance the classical with the colloquial, to not only make these poems contemporary, but also to make them oral so they can be spoken aloud: and that was my final test for each of them.

The titles I have given them are my own (they are untitled in the original) as a way of clarifying the area of their meaning, and they have come out of the inner fabric of each poem, often in relationship to its central image. We wanted to minimize commentary and footnotes, so this was an obvious way of doing so, letting the poems as much as possible speak for themselves, as themselves, as they would to any literate Chinese reader. In giving them titles, too, I have seen them taking their place alongside the *I Ching*, the Tarot and the runes, which they are in every way equal to. They are doorways of realization, colouring themselves as inner landscapes through their imagery, as well as being catalysts for visualization and meditation, as they invite us deeper into our own seeing and understanding, and into the pictures of truth our own lives are always giving us, as we learn to read them for what they are.

But since I want the last word to be Kuan Yin's, not my own, I want to finish with a story I found quoted by Vicki Noble in her *Motherpeace Tarot*. A Chinese nun was describing to John Blofeld how she makes space within herself so that Kuan Yin can appear to her. She tells him:

> With your mind make everything empty. There's nothing there, you say. And you see it like that – nothing, emptiness . . . Then there's the sea, and the moon has risen – full, round, white . . . You stare at the moon a long, long time feeling calm, happy. Then the moon gets smaller, but brighter and brighter until you see it as a pearl or a seed so bright you can only just bear to look at it. The pearl starts to grow, and before you know what's happened, it's Kuan Yin herself standing up against the sky . . .

You might like to try it for yourself now, to make it your own.

And may the peace, the clear-sighted wisdom and the laughter of Her Being be with you, as we face our futures:

> Look up at Heaven now – it has a Milky Way of stars . . .
> I tell you recognition and awareness will come in time.

Using the Poems as Divination

The 100 poems which follow are used extensively for divination purposes in Chinese temples and homes around the world. The usual method, as described in Martin's introduction to the poems *(pages 97–100)*, is either to open the book at random and allow the poem to speak to your circumstances or to cast the divination sticks.

Perhaps the simplest way of using the poems for inspiration is to just open the book and allow whichever poem you happen upon to speak to you. Before doing so, try to be in as calm and meditative a frame of mind as possible. Sit still for a few minutes, contemplating the issue about which you are seeking guidance. Allow yourself to abandon any attempt at control and then make your random choice of poem. For at the heart of such divination systems is a belief in the importance of randomness. In going to the oracles for help, you are abandoning all attempts to reason or rationalize your way through a situation. Instead, in true Taoist terms, you are allowing the flow of Nature, the Way of the Tao, to speak to you by giving up your somewhat feeble attempts to make sense of your place in the cosmos. Thus any attempt to control which poem you end up with is wrong. You must abandon yourself to chance in order that the Tao can break through your self-defences and speak to you.

For the Chinese user of the poems, this is done through the divination sticks. Thin strips of bamboo or wood, they are numbered from 1 to 100. Placed in a special container, inscribed with auspicious characters, they are shaken until one or more falls out. The numbers on these sticks are the numbers of the divination poem you should refer to. Since most readers will not have access to a set of divination sticks, we have devised an alternative method which offers a deeper way of using the poems than just opening a page. This is why on the next two pages you will find the numbers 1 to 100 set out in totally random fashion, one for each of the poems. We suggest that you close your eyes and place your finger on a spot on the page and then see what number you have come up with. This replicates what the divination sticks themselves do for the devout user.

But don't just do this once. For the divination sticks have an illuminating quality rather than a prescriptive quality. Chinese divination is not fatalistic. It never tells you what will happen as if there were no choice. All it ever does is indicates what is *likely* to happen if you continue along the path you are currently on. It always remains within your power to change the course of the future by altering what you do and to some extent who you are.

This is why we suggest that you make three choices of numbers, using the random finger to page method. Then look up the three poems and allow them to speak to you about your past, your present and your future.

Let us give you an example. You are wanting to know whether a relationship you have had should continue and whether it will be one which will last. You have weighed all the factors and you simply cannot decide whether to continue or not. So you turn to the goddess for help. Choosing randomly, you end up with poem 23, poem 57 and poem 44. The first relates to your past, the second to the present and the third to the future.

Your past is perhaps captured in poem 23's picture of you as someone who has tried to climb to the moon! You have overstretched yourself maybe, for all that you sought for has not happened – the Gate of Heaven is still shut to you. Frustration and over-ambition are indicated.

Your present is captured in no. 57, possibly in the advice to talk in depth with one who can understand – avoid 'small talk'; 'let's put our thoughts together'. You need to talk this through with someone who takes you seriously.

Your potential for the future is outlined in no. 44. The advice is, take your time, don't blow it through haste, nor fear that if you do take time, all will be lost. It is also hopeful – see the first line.

In the end, the divination offers no definitive answer. It cannot. What it does is focuses your own thoughts and suggests possible ways forward. Ultimately it is still you who will make the future, but perhaps you can now do so guided by the insights of the goddess. You have overreached yourself and it has not come to be as you hoped. You need to take time and to talk it through with someone you trust. Then you must sort out what you really want and only then move. If you follow this, you are likely to eventually arrive at the state you want with the one you want.

We wish you well in your dialogue with the goddess, who, as we have pointed out earlier, is not really a miracle worker or a magician, but the compassionate companion who works best with what you are or what you could become.

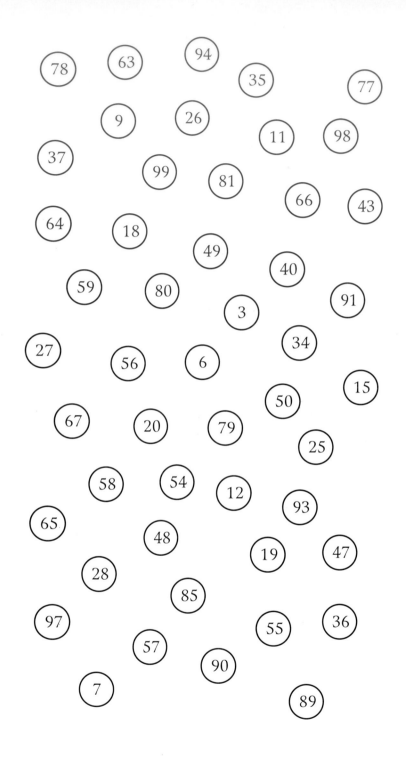

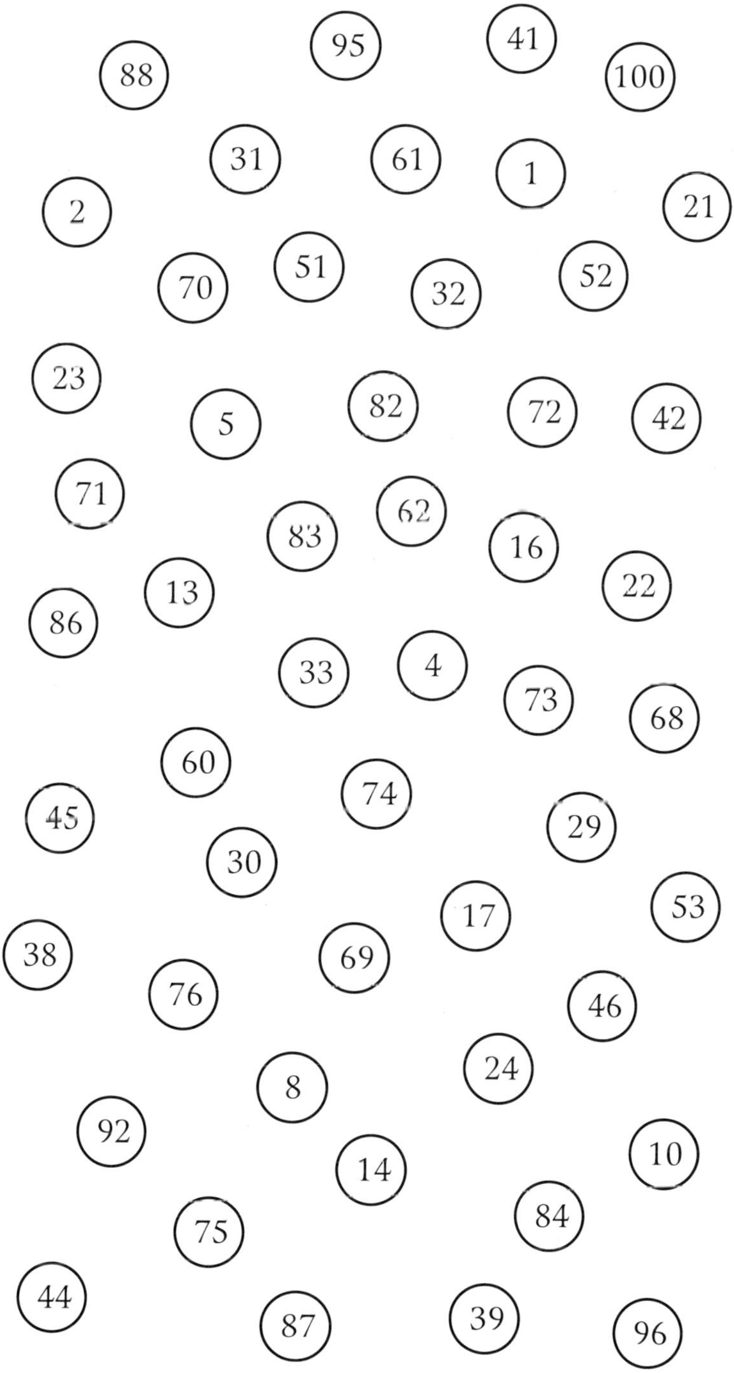
95
41
88
100
31
61
1
2
21
70
51
32
52
23
5
82
72
42
71
62
83
16
22
13
86
33
4
73
68
60
74
45
29
30
17
53
38
69
76
46
24
8
92
10
14
84
75
44
39
87
96

ⓖ ⓖ ⓖ ⓖ ⓖ ⓖ ⓖ ⓖ

KUAN YIN

The Quatrains: 1–100

HEAVEN'S DOOR OPENING,
EARTH'S ERUPTING BIRTH

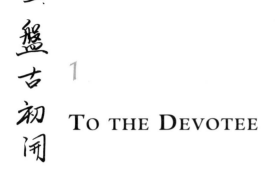

1

To the Devotee

From the beginning of Creation, everything had meaning:
The lucky day brings everything fruiting to ripeness . . .
Then revelation comes – and don't take it lightly –
The pure-hearted being will be graced by the Divine One.

二.

鯨
魚
未
変

2

THE FLYING ONE

The whale stays waiting and watching in the waters . . .

Don't try to reach too high, or fly too far –

One day your royal, inner eye will lighten and open

And then you'll salmon-leap the Dragon gate gorge in one!

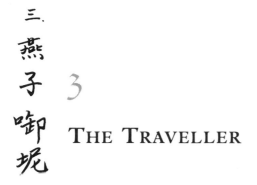

三.
燕
子
啣
坭

3

THE TRAVELLER

Wind-blown, and rain-soaked, he battles back along the road
He comes as straight as a swallow flying back to her nest –
She builds her muddy house like a rampart to stay dry
But then it falls apart, dissolving, like a sigh all over again.

四.

古鏡重圓

4

STARTING OVER

Way back, a mirror was shattered: now it can be healed again:
She can leave her husband, and she can choose another –
Setting up a new nest, they can make their lives complete,
And it will breeze a good magic and ease to all their children.

五.
錐
地
求
泉

5

IN THE DARKNESS

Dig deep into the earth where the spring water gushes,

Through sheer pain and labour, seek to win through –

In a place like this, then, you come across a true friend . . .

And seeing each other again (*it's you!*) you both touch Heaven.

六.
投
岩
銅
鳥

6

BE YOURSELF (SAYS THE POET)

Go and live in a copper mine underground with the birds!

Be in harmony with yourself and all the other paths –

Everyone goes their own way and tries as best they can,

And no one can cover the whole of Heaven and Earth's expanse.

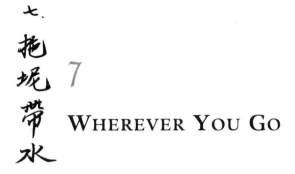

7

WHEREVER YOU GO

The restless, surging waves bring troubles in your way –
The streams are clogged with soil and clay from the mountain,
And the one who tries to function beyond the Great Wall
Has not yet come home to himself at all.

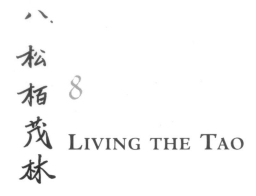

8

LIVING THE TAO

In the forest, the pines and cypresses grow straight up
And neither rain nor wind, snow or frost can harm them –
One day to come you'll see what it all was for . . .
And these will be the pillars of the temple of community.

九.
皎
月
當
通

9

IN THE CIRCLE'S ROUND

A true man doesn't allow emotions to distract him,

Let this understanding guide and open your right mind:

Then your heart can be filled with light, pure and sublime,

Like the full moon shining in a cloudless night sky . . .

十.

持燈覓火

10

It's You

There's a treasury full of jade and jewels: it is in you
Don't go searching far from home for it – it's here,
Or you're like the man with a lantern looking for light,
And can't you see what a total waste of time *that* is?

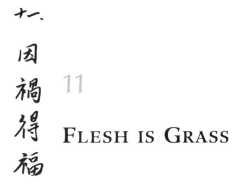

11

FLESH IS GRASS

No success in the market place lasts for long,
And even among family, there are always ructions . . .
With luck, the arrow grounds the vanishing liquid deer
And the wisest person around is found to guide the way.

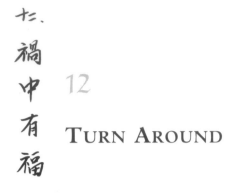

12

TURN AROUND

The line between exalted and debased is very thin –
Reach out and talk with the man who lives near the mountain gate,
He says: the messenger *himself* will be met with good news . . .
What your heart centres wholly on will open the door.

十三.

龍
門
得
通

13

LUCKY ONE

You were born into a privileged and notorious family,

Your destiny offers you everything in ease and comfort

The Emperor will present you with a silken gold sash,

And your charisma will be as boundless as the four seas.

十四.

仙
鶴
離
籠

14

IN THE CLEAR

Like the beautiful undying crane that breaks free

You can slip the bars of your cage and journey on through –

North, South, East and West nothing is obstructing you –

The *chun*,* the wise one, can rise to the highest Ninth Heaven.

* *chun* = wise one, person

INTO THE GREEN

Thirsty and footsore, as you walk in the heat of the day
Sudden disasters come out of the sky, out of nowhere –
Like a bird whose nest has plummeted out of a tree
To find yourself in peace, go deep into the wilderness.

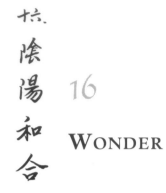

16

WONDER

This is not the moment for a long face or frown,
Throw your fears out of your mind and let the joy in –
It's like finding a piece of jade in the middle of a dungheap:
The workman stands and wipes the dirt off it in wonder.

十七、

畫餅充飢

17

FOOD FOR PRAYER

Don't give your ears to intrigue and scandal

Spend your time chanting to the Buddha of Release . . .

If you give credence to these sillinesses

You're like a man trying to feed off pictures of cake!

十八、
陰陽消長

18

BEYOND CLASS OR CREED

Golden crow-sun sets and sinks, as white rabbit-moon rises
Day and night have circled each other since time immemorial,
And since you know this, follow the Way as it helps everyone –
Scholar or workman, shop girl and businessman all benefit.

19

BREATHE

The ferryboat is flung through the white gorge waters,
The wind and the waves surge and crash – but oh why?
You can't find a calm centredness in this mess –
So wait until the groundswell ebbs and dies away . . .

20

After the Grey

When the teeming rain stops, the clear sky is a joy –
Jade hare moon and gold bird sun slowly, slowly brighten
The tangled times are gone, the joy-time is to come –
And with just one leap you can clear the Dragon Gate again.

二十、
陰
陽
道
合

21

TOGETHER

The Ultimate and Heaven together make the yin-yang way,

And the melding of man and woman is joyously the same –

So the dragon shall coil and twist with the snake . . .

And together they shall come into the same dreaming Garden.

二十二.

旱逢甘雨

22

DRYNESS AND UNDERSTANDING

When drought comes on the rice crop, it all withers and dies:

Thank Heaven then that a rainstorm bursts, soaking it –

Flowers, fruit, trees and grass are all fed to their roots,

And the beginning of knowing is that rain is worth everything.

23 IMMORTALITY

手板仙桂

You try to climb the healing tree to the Palace of the Moon,
But sadly the Gate of Heaven is not open – even for you,
But the fact that you tried will travel far and wide . . .
And everyone will smile and enjoy the flowers in their gardens.

24

BEYOND REASON

No reason: then a row makes your home no place to be,

Ah, we are like fading blossom drifting on an endless sea

Ask anyone if grace stays with those who are misaligned –

All that's left is a heap of problems in all you're doing.

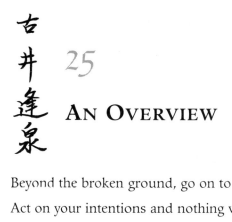

25

AN OVERVIEW

Beyond the broken ground, go on to finish all that's to be done

Act on your intentions and nothing will be wrong –

A broad heart can encompass every imaginable thing,

And things like this, seen from over you, bring real blessing.

虚
名
之
象

26

ILLUSION

Wild rumours run up and down among your colleagues,
From the blue edge of the horizon, guidance comes –
And what it seems to promise is *you shall be honoured*
But it doesn't stop you from tripping over on the ground!

27

IN PERFECT TIME

You structure, you plan it, you think it out to the detail
But it's all held back and you can't go forward –
When you really need it, and the time's right, a wise one comes:
Then the walls of your house will be fit for you to dwell in.

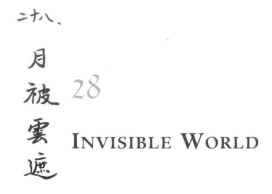

28

INVISIBLE WORLD

On the eastern edge, the moon rises, so full of grace
And though it's hidden, out of sight, it still *is* . . .
It can be either full or waning, but it goes on its way:
Loudmouths will always curse, and their words are nothing.

二十九.

定
劍
出
匣

29

GOLD

The precious sword is drawn out, and it gleams . . .
It is untouched by dust and burnished, like gold –
Now the wise one goes forward to see what can be done,
And to have nobility like this is to be envied by everyone.

斗.
安
份
守
己

30

KUAN YIN'S WARNING

My advice to you is please don't be over-ambitious,
The white crane must beware the secret arrow in the mist
Pulling at firewood, you can uncover a hissing snake –
And one bite from it could bring complete disaster.

31

RELAXATION

A wise one's way of life is relaxed and spacious,
Pause here and breathe; take time to drink your tea,
It's pointless wearing yourself out with what you're doing –
You can be certain then that no dis-ease will be drawn to you.

廿二、

剖
石
見
玉

32

THE HEART OF IT

The journey goes on far, far into the unknown –

And you can't know whether there's jade in the heart of the rock

One day, a man will chisel it free into the daylight . . .

So be calm; you know, it's been there since the beginning of time.

33

PRESENCE

Don't you understand that everything *here* is what matters?

To find the jade, go beyond the boundaries of your skin –

You can't do better than wait for the *chun* to manifest,

I tell you, this is the best thing – no question about it.

廿四.

紅
日
當
空

34

MORALITY

In everything you do, live for the truth –
Your words should be clear and your actions substantial,
Don't have ideas in your heart that are not discernible,
Stand at the centre like the bright rays pouring from the sun!

35

WITH LOVE

With love, let a new breeze blow through your house –
The Way is cleared by *Te*, Virtue, as it always was . . .
So clear your path of the harsh growths that separate you,
When all Three can be in harmony, you'll know what's to come.

36

KUAN YIN'S ASSURANCE

For the moment there's trouble, but don't be distressed,
Please know that the riches of the earth await you . . .
A clever monkey wants freedom, even from a golden chain,
He's longing to find his way back to his mountain cave.

風搖燈燭

卅七.

37

THE RECLUSE

Don't wander with your head up at the wrong time,
It's not a good idea to light a candle in the wind –
Don't try to do things here – get yourself away,
Live like a hermit on retreat, live in peace.

廿八.

雲霧遮月

38

IN PASSING

Waiting for words to come from the moonlit sky . . .
Suddenly, dark clouds drift across like chilling smoke
But don't let your heart be darkened like them –
The moment always passes and gladness will return.

39

UNREADY

The thought comes, drop by drop, from the edge of Heaven
It pleads with you but its message can't penetrate –
It's as if a dull stone could become a shimmering mirror,
Be like a wise worker – and don't waste your skills.

40 KING AND QUEEN

As the sunset's red revolves, the moon's light is born,
Yin breathes up – yang sighs, suffusing everything . . .
Like a woman thinking about finding a good man –
If she's careful with her heart, she will be blessed.

叱

認
賊 41
作
子

THE DEMON OF HIDING

Beware of those charming silver-tongued devils,
It's as if you'd welcomed a thief as your son –
Don't hide anything now, or you'll regret it . . .
A false act now could bring you years of pain.

42

UNDESERVED

Grace comes from the Heavenly Court with all its faces,
Honour follows with its blessing and there's no hitch –
You use it, and everything goes well for you . . .
All life, you see (can you?) *is caught up in Heaven.*

43

DIVINITY

Heaven and earth suffuse all life in perfect harmony,
Everything living looks to itself to develop and improve,
All that is created has beauty and delight in it –
And sages and Godly people emanate it all . . .

四十四.

棋
逢
敵
手

44

THE CHESS GAME

For the first time, you meet someone on your level –
In this game, it's so hard to know how to move . . .
Why? Because one false step, and you blow it
So think before you know what you're going to do.

45

SWEETNESS

The young and the old overcome the tough and the hard,
Nurture happiness, and the Great Gates of Goodness will open –
And this is true – why? *Because it brings the right reading,*
And then it's like slaking your thirst by drinking nectar.

四快.

枯
木
生
花

46

THE HELPER

The wise one's advice is: first of all, do nothing

Take care not to try anything at all . . . stay still –

Wait for someone to come who can guide the work for you:

After times like this, the dying tree has flowered again.

四十七.

錦上添花

47 THE WORLD TEACHER

The first blossoms are freshly woven on silk . . .
Carried along by a horse there is happiness and fortune,
It's never too late for people to speak well of you –
Make the grade, and become a teacher to us all.

四十八

鷗鵬興變

48 ORDINARY AND EXTRAORDINARY

A simple forest bird becomes a great rock in autumn,

Such good luck and blessing it goes beyond words . . .

It soars vast distances at all the sky's edges –

It goes beyond all bounds, beyond all you have known.

四十九.

水
結
成
冰

49

WISDOM

Heaven below zero, the earth freezing, water congealing
So what is the point of being famous and well-known?
It's best to wait and see beyond all of this –
Until the real time comes, and your eye can see clearly.

50

THAWING

The nation employs the wise one to travel,

The sails begin to fill out, stretch and tauten –

And now with the wind breezing, the ship begins to move,

And layer after layer of treasure is found waiting!

五十一.

人
人
愁
熱

AS THE SPIRIT MOVES

Throughout the blazing long hot days of summer
Everyone seems permanently sad, depressed and grieving –
Yes, Heaven and Earth affect the human mind . . .
And the gentle cool wafting of the breeze is soothing.

五七、

貪求費力

52

THE TIME WASTER

Spending time looking for the moon in a pool of water

Is a waste of time – it's an effort to no purpose –

So don't speak ill thought-out words or tattle –

It's stupid to think this will touch anyone but you!

五十三、

龍
吟
虎
嘯

53

KUAN YIN'S PROMISE

It's unwise to always follow your own mind,

It sounds like a dragon's drone or a tiger's laugh –

Look up at Heaven now – it has a Milky Way of stars . . .

I tell you recognition and awareness will come in time.

五十四.

夢
中
得
寶

54

PRICKING THE BUBBLE

Illusion, a fantasy, you wake; you realize *none of it's true,*
But it's true that good things are heard in your conscience
What is there in marriage? And in superficial health?
Look beyond it, or you'll stay disheartened and bitter.

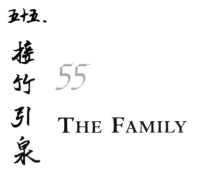

五十五.

55

THE FAMILY

A good father teaches his son, who teaches his children
Heaven will then take care of everything that's needed –
Your parents will blossom and find their garden . . .
Ah, let them drink and sleep, not hemmed in with your worries.

56

BALANCE

The stream bubbles and sings over its bed of pebbles,
The wind is keen, the moon bright, the high ones are glad –
And after asking about the path of all your striving, see this:
The scent of the forest flowers comes from the right conditions.

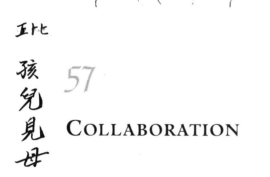

57 COLLABORATION

Don't let the slough of small talk addle your brain,

Isn't it better to honour yourself and earn respect?

A wise one doesn't remember a person's age, and shouldn't,

You feel the same as I do – let's put our thoughts together.

卦八.

守常待時

58

YOUR OWN AUTHORITY

Take down this clear guidance; a wise one's advice,

It's not for you to go around everywhere looking for it –

Cut loose – stand back, and make your own decisions . . .

Get yourself away and find space, without invasion.

王十九.

守苗
隨
時

59 THE RIGHT PLACE

Ascend – it's vital you hole up in your tower,

It's like being in a forest surrounded by thorns . . .

Heaven's highest wise one decides the web of fate –

Don't take on things beyond the reach of your powers . . .

60

INFERNO

The fire swells with heat when it's stoked up with fuel,

It ravages a tract of land – and then it turns on you,

It's no use; you're going to burn in your own blood,

Do you think your money can buy you out?

六十一.

守苗隨時

61

THE PRIZE OF LIFE

At sunrise, prayers are chanted moon-set, there's singing
Take part in whatever's happening, but laugh too – laugh
Grief comes out of nowhere, and you turn your face away
But shout out for the prize of life, join in with the note!

六十二.

神佛暗佑

62

THE MAN HIMSELF

Throughout the day and night, the Buddha protects us –
He clarifies the way as if through his own body . . .
Following such a wise one, to meet him is luck itself!
When you meet true richness, unbelievable wealth comes.

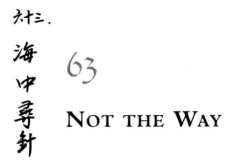

六十三.

海中尋針

63

NOT THE WAY

When the day to go by boat comes, the compass is lost –
We're sailing in mid-ocean now, trying to find it,
As if now is the time we *have* to find it –
But that's a waste of energy, a waste of compassion.

六十四.

魚
遭
羅
網

64

FATE

The fish swims in muddied jade green water
Surrounded on all sides by a trawler net;
He thinks that if he wriggles, he can escape –
And fate says yes, OK: and equally, no: no way.

六十五、

割
肉
成
瘡

65

WAKEFULNESS

Don't rest on your laurels with what you've got;

It's neither 'bad', at this time, nor is it 'good'.

Don't cut a part of yourself off to make a patch,

Don't react like this to make a change . . .

66

SPEEDING

The man's in a hurry and the horses are in danger on the road,
To lose a company of soldiers means you're both in trouble
It's like a broken vessel, blown through the rushing gorge . . .
Sunlight fades the blossoms, and Heaven sends down frost.

67

THE MIDDLE WAY

The *chun* takes care to maintain the golden mean,

Don't add to it, resist it, or fawn to it either –

Stay with truth, standing awake, putting others first –

You need consciousness and grounding to shine as you are.

68

BLESSING

Open your doors to blessing – it doesn't come every day,
Store up goodness and open the gates wide to glory!
It's a good time for you farmers, couples, and families –
And at last the sick are freed into a new lease of life.

六十九.

69

FIVE SEASONS

A plum tree stands alone on a hill of its own,

Its petals drop, its branches wither, its sap falls low . . .

And yet spring comes with all its vibrancy in spite of frost

And the beauty and the life return to the flowers (see them).

七十.

蜜蜂採花

70

THE CHANCE OF THE MORNING

The coming of the morning is like a bee among the flowers,

He buzzes and roves wherever he needs to go . . .

Springtime passes and the flowers no longer blossom,

Pained in your heart, there's nowhere to go or stay.

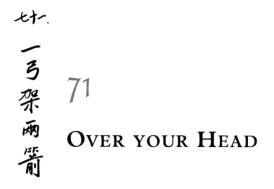

71

OVER YOUR HEAD

Who can grasp the Dragon of the *Nineteenth* Level?
A woman shouldn't marry or live with two husbands –
How in all honesty can one bow handle two arrows?
It's sad, but dragons and horses just can't get on.

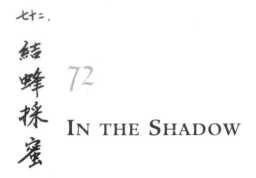

七十二.

72

IN THE SHADOW

We use the bees to make sweet honey
Yet we dread getting the sting in their tail –
Naturally, there are other ways to make things to live;
Your seeing is cloudy and hidden as if in a poisonous wood.

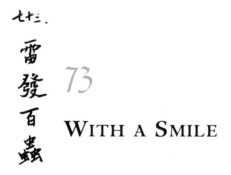

七十三.

雷
發
百
蟲

73

WITH A SMILE

Spring's coming unfortunately brings out all the bugs,
Metamorphosing themselves they flourish from the mud –
In winter they all return from where they started
At dawn they get going like a dragon off its lead!

七十四.

似
鵠
投
水

74

BEING WHO YOU ARE

A snow goose snags itself inside a cage –
Wanting to change itself, this is *not* the way through
Every way *away from herself* she can't escape . . .
This reading is the saddest and truest one of all.

七十五.

抱
虎
過
山

75

THE WRONG WAY UP

It's not a good idea to climb a mountain with a tiger,
You're wobbly, you're nervous, every move you make is tense
Suddenly something you remember could help you now –
And if you do what you learnt then you won't fall foul.

76

THE LOVERS

A fish and a dragon in a river thought, 'We'll live together.'
They hid deep in the depths, waiting for their time . . .
Staying out of trouble, one morning they'll escape –
And they'll leap the gate in one, into the Palace of Ecstasy.

七十七.

夢中得寶

77

IN REALITY

In a dream, you're told how to find a great fortune!
Your reputation and wealth lie beyond your grasp –
Hardships exist, but they don't have to bring you down,
A wise one will guide you, then you will be laughing.

七十八.

平善用事

78

SIMPLICITY

Don't boil up the water so hot it turns white –
Neither frothing, or too cool – let it warm gently,
Do what Heaven wants not what someone else decides,
Make do with what you have: it's the milk of human life.

79

THE GUARDIANS

Lying to your protector-guide doesn't lead to peace,
He finds peace for you – but you give nothing back;
Don't forget that what the holy ones advise is right
Don't treat their bread with meaningless disrespect.

八十.
貴人接引

80

REVERSED

You want to become immortal at once, so you study it –
And before you know it one morning you're made Emperor.
Heaven, the sun and moon all shine brightly down on you,
And sincerity, in your name, spreads across the four seas.

八十一.
梧
桐
落
葉

81

THE UNKNOWN STORY

In autumn, the leaves flake from the phoenix tree
And the travellers come home like birds migrating . . .
The workmen thank Heaven who is their protection –
And a vessel full of treasure is borne home on the wind.

小七.

火
裏
生
蓮

82

THE WATER LILY

Fluorescent orange flames blaze with a heat like Heaven,
Scorching everything in their path – but not the water lily;
It seems as if it must die – but it isn't even touched –
All its tendrils and flowers come back on the other side.

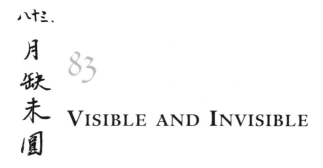

八十三.

月缺未圓

83

VISIBLE AND INVISIBLE

You can't see the moon in its early new days
But isn't it radiant, gold and round, nevertheless?
Wait until mid-month for the Lighting of the Night –
And then its brightness fills the whole circle of the sky.

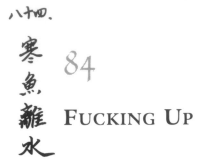

84 FUCKING UP

Virtue and a good name can be ruined by wrong doing,
Take care; in a streak of good luck, the chill can come –
The drunk, pissed in his cups, has nowhere he can lean
And the pine tree is a shadow in the dreams of liars.

八十五.

春
尽
花
开

85

AWAKENING

The clouds part, but the way is misty on the mountain:

All of Creation becomes a circle when the moon is full –

When you wake up, your fictional dreams and fantasies die,

And the wise one will lead you to the true, real Paradise.

八十六.

上朝見帝

86

SHAKEN

Spring flowers shine with a Paradise-glow,

Thousands of wagons arrive here stacked with wealth,

You find your way to the highest accolade as if on a wave,

And if you're lucky, it's like a thunderclap that bumps you down!

八十七、

淘沙見金

DANGER MOUNTAIN

The climber reaches the middle of the peak in a day,
But what are you doing here? It's dangerous –
Looking up ahead, he prays that Heaven will protect him,
And then the crag in front of him opens like a cave.

THE FACE OF POWER

Carve a wooden tiger to guard your door:

Its teeth are bared, but actually it harms no one –

It seems to do the trick, but doesn't stop anyone else –

So you can relax and be yourself while you're out being human.

八十九.

89

THE JACKPOT

The one who goes out to try it has great luck –

The way the highest quality jade isn't visible in the rock,

Yes, indeed, you should get advice from a wise one . . .

The time has come to find happiness as it's always been found.

九十.
功名成就

90

RAINBOW MOUNTAIN

An unexpected prompting comes from Heaven –
Mount T'ai gives its riches completely unexpectedly –
However, it's good for you to know what could happen to you;
The wise one has ways and means to help you travel on.

九十一、

前途顕達

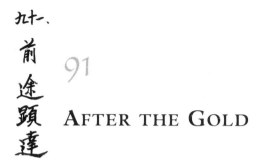

91

AFTER THE GOLD

It's good to be relaxed and go out to the people,

Really think about your work – and search for happiness,

A great path comes in front of you, and Heaven opens the gate;

And then? Do all you can for those who haven't what you have.

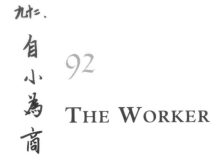

92

THE WORKER

From his youth his interest was in means of trading,
He had wealth and prosperity he never even touched –
He did it himself using his wits to reach his ends,
He came out of the masses, and he became Prime Minister.

九十三.

鸞鳳被雨

93 THE PHOENIX

The fabulous fire-bird's wings are both dripping wet,
He makes the opening but even the little birds outdo him –
One day the sun will come back and all shall be well . . .
His plumage will be resplendent like a great king or queen.

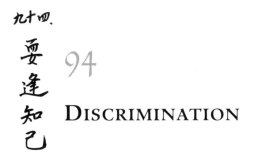

94 DISCRIMINATION

The sage's son doesn't mix with mean-minded people,

Their lives aren't clear, they're like a muddied pool –

The lute's sound can only be savoured by an adept . . .

Stay in your calm, and you'll be able to carry it through.

志氣功名

九十五.

95

REACHING THE END

To honour your goal you need to work at it every day,
And now the lure of wine and thighs is hard to overcome –
If you see the true gold, then a wise one will speak for you:
Wealth, good luck, happiness and a high place are all waiting.

96

THE BEACON OF TRUTH

The precious pagoda: there's no need to keep searching –
It refracts its multifaceted light in every direction . . .
The sage says: be willing to work, pray, and bow down –
And if you do, Heaven can bless you with every reward.

97

THE LIVING IMAGE

A candle in the breeze casts flickering shadows,

Flurried and blurred they fan out like willow-flowers . . .

The boy adrift at sea pleads to be picked up –

Just learn to be true to yourself, like a raft on the water.

98 TRAPPED

I ask you to look at your business slowly and carefully,
It's not a good idea to be lazy – it's provocative . . .
It's like when a handful of birds are caught in a snare,
They have to learn to see the subtleties of the trap.

99

BURN OUT

To try and rein in a flogged horse is too late,

To be half burnt-out alive, with the other half dead –

It's like having the whole house on fire around you,

The summer rains will come and dissolve it all to mud.

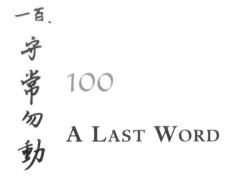

100

A Last Word

Buddha and the gods speak the highest truth in oracles,
The stupid man lies and turns his back on it all –
Dear Reader: I beg you to go the whole way with this . . .
There's no time left to hope for better things.

KUAN   LOOK   gaze with awakened eyes
        regard the
SHI   WORLD   at the Age that is dawning
        turning with
YIN   SOUND   scored at the heart of song –
reaching above
           forever
              reaching beyond

INDEX

allegorical level 98–9
Amaterasu (Shinto goddess) 47, 49
Amida Buddha 20
Ananda (in Buddhism) 19
ancestors, concern about 99
animal husbandry, concern about 99
Armed Kuan Yin 42–3
Avalokitesvara 4–5, 43, 45, 47–8, 49
axe, symbolism of 40–1

beauty, function of, in poems 97,
    101–7
Bodhisattva xii, 3, 17, 41
Bon 23
'The Bridge of Fukien' 80–6
Buddha 4, 40
Buddhavatamsaka Sutra 31–2
Buddhism:
    in China 14, 23–5
    in Japan 43
    in Kuan Yin symbols 41
    patriarchy in 17, 18–19
    rivalry with Taoism 17–22
business, concern about 99

Cave of the Tidal Sound, Pu To Shan
    33–4
Chang Tao Ling 17
Chang-an 22, 24
change:
    and choice 114
    as natural process 110
change of fortune 86–7
Cheng Ming Ching 8
Ch'i Shan (Chou Sacred Mountain) 12,
    14
Chiang Chih Ch'i 30, 63–5
Chien shou, chien yen Kuan Shih Yin Pusa
    ta pei hsin to lo ni Ching (Sutra of
    the Thousand-Hand and
    Thousand-Eyed Kuan Yin of the
    Great Compassionate Heart) 32
child-bearer role 38, 47–8

child-giver role xi, xii, 38
Chin Shi Huang Ti 10
Chinese Buddhism xi–xii, 14
Chinese mythology 9–11
Chinese poetry, structure 101, 108,
    110
Ching Ching (Chinese Christian priest)
    24, 31
choice, and change 114
Christianity xi, 22–5
Chu Tzu ('Songs of the South') 13, 15
Chujo Hime 46
chun 108, 110
The Classic of the Mountains and the Seas
    15
compassion 26, 50–1, 86–7
Confucianism 13, 19
creation stories 57–62
crow, symbolism of 41
cycle (Buddhist), breaking xii

danger xii
divination, use of poems xiii, 97–101
    example 114
divination books 100, 103
divination sticks 97–8, 100, 113–14
Divine, immanence, assertion of 109
divine feminine xiii, 9–25, 51–3, 105
divine revelation, poems as 99–100,
    106

earth mother figure 10
Egyptian influence, on Christianity 23,
    25
11-headed Kannon 47
emergence, of Kuan Yin 23–5

family, concern about 99
farming, concern about 99
fate 86–7
female, transformation from male xii,
    6–25, 32, 47–50, 105
female deities 17

feminine:
    assertion of, in processes of Nature 109
    divine xiii, 9–25, 51–3, 105
finances, concern about 99
Five Bushels sect 16–17
format, of Chinese poetry 101, 110
Fu Hsi 9
future, guidance 115

Goddess of Compassion xi
guidance, from poems 108, 115
gylanic world, in Chinese mythology 9–11

Han Shan Te Ch'ing 36–7
Hangchow 28–9, 33, 101, 102–4
'The Healing of Chao Ying' 88–9
history, of poems 101–5
Horse Voice Kuan Yin 47
Horse-headed Kannon 47
hou, ridden by Kuan Yin 41
Hsi Tien monastery 33
Hsiang Shan, monastery at 30, 32–3
Hsuan Tsang 8, 89, 103–4
Hua Hu Ching (Record of Lao Tzu's Discourses with Foreigners) 18
Hua Yen Ching (Flower Ornament Sutra) 31–2

I Ching 12, 100–1, 106–9, 111
illness, concern about 99
images, of Kuan Yin 37–42
incarnation, in Japanese Kannon tradition 45–6
intercessor role xi, 3
interpretation 107
    according to 14 basic areas of concern 99
    example 114
Islam 23

Japan, Kuan Yin as Kannon ix, 25, 43–50
Journey to the West (Wu Cheng'en) 103–4

Kannon, Japanese Kuan Yin xi, 25, 43–50, 51
Kannon of the Easy Delivery 47–8
Karura 45
Korea xi, 25, 43, 51
Koyasu Kannon 47
Kuan Shi Yin, symbolism of name 106, 125
Kuan Yin of the Southern Ocean 41
Kumarajiva (master translator) 5–6, 7

Lao Tzu 14, 18

legal cases, concern about 99
The Life of the Ta Pei Bodhisattva of Hsiang Shan 63–5
local deities, absorption into mainstream beliefs 17, 25–6
lost relatives or friends, concern about 99
lost thing, finding, concern about 99
lotus, symbolism of 37–8, 40
Lotus Sutra 3, 4–6, 7–8, 17, 23, 26, 37–9, 40, 43, 50
Lung Men caves, nr Loyang 8
Lung Nu 38

Madonna representations, influence on Kuan Yin images 24–5, 38
Mahayana Buddhism 3–4, 17
male, transformation to female xii, 6–25, 32, 47–50, 105
Man-Ho Kwok 99
Manichaeism 23
Mao Shan Taoism 18
marriage, concern about 99
meditation, poems as catalyst 111
Miao Fa Lien Hua Ching see Lotus Sutra
Miao Shan 27–8, 30, 32–3, 38, 39–40, 63–78
Mikichi Okada 49–50
miracles of Kuan Yin 86–93
miraculous deliverance from the sea story 78–86
models, of female deities 24–5
'Monkey' 89–93, 104
mother goddess culture 11–13
moving house, concern about 99

Nature:
    assertion of the feminine in 109
    law of 109
    Spirit in 107
Nestorian Christianity 22–4
New Religious Movements, in Japan 48–9
Nua Kua 9, 12
numbers 1–100 114, *116–17*

Old Grandmother of the Mountain (T'ai Shan) 10, 20
100 divination sticks 97–8, 100
One Who Hears the Cries of the World xii, 5, 53
opening *see* random opening

pairing and contrast, in poems 109
patriarchy:
    in Buddhism 17, 18–19
    in Confucianism 13, 19
    in religions xiii, 18–19, 21
    in societies 11

peacock's eyes legend 41, 62
personal release or salvation 16–17
poems:
    levels of 97–8
    link with temples 101–2
    poetic level 98, 99–100
    structure 101, 108, 110
    use 97–101
Potalaka (mystical island) 31–2
Prajna (Indian monk) 24, 31
pregnancy, concern about 99
Princess Miao Shan 27–8, 30, 32–3,
    38, 39–40, 63–78
Protector of All Life 41
Pu To Shan 30–6, 102, 103

quatrain format, in poems 110
Queen Mother of the East 11–12
Queen Mother of Heaven 13–14
Queen Mother of the West 11–12,
    14–16, 17, 19, 20, 21, 35–6

rabbit, symbolism of 41
random opening 113
reincarnation 86
rhyme, in poems 110
rhythm, in poems 110
rosary 37, 38, 40
runes 111
Ryushin Kannon 45

Sacred Mountains xi
Saddharma Pundarika Sutra (Sutra of the
    Lotus of the Wondrous Law) *see*
    Lotus Sutra
Sakyamuni Buddha xi
Sanjusangen-do Temple, Kyoto 44
sea goddesses, adopted in Kuan Yin
    26, 41
sea stories 78–86
Sekai Kyusei Kyo 49
sequence, in poems 109
shamanism 11, 13, 15–16, 23, 100
    in Kuan Yin symbols 39
    re-emergence as Taoism 13, 16, 17
suppression 19
Shan Ts'ai 38
Shang Ch'ing texts 17
Shang Tien Chu monastery 28, 33
Sheng Hsi Ming 33
Shinto New Religious Movements 49
Shintoism ix, 47–50
Shotoku, Prince 43
sickness xi, xii
'Songs of the South' *see Chu Tzu*
Spirit, in Nature 107
spread, of worship of Kuan Yin 25–37

statues:
    at Hangchow 28, 30, 33
    of female deities 23–4
suicide 33–4
Surangama Sutra 8

Ta Pei statue 63
Ta sheng li ch'u po lo to ching 24
Taema-dera temple, Yamato 46
T'ai Shan (Taoist Sacred Mountain)
    9–10, 19–20
    goddess of 10, 12
Taisan-ji Temple, Kyoto 48
Tao Te Ching 12, 13, 14, 106, 108–9,
    110
Taoism xi, xii, 23
    re-emergence of shamanism in 13,
    16, 17
    rivalry with Buddhism 17–22
Tarot 107, 111
Te (virtue), assertion of 109
temples, link with poems 101–2
Theravada Buddhism 3
33 manifestations of Kannon 44–5
thoughts, focusing 115
*The Thousand-Armed, Thousand-Eyed
    Kuan Yins* 39–41, 44
Three August Ones 9
three-headed Kuan Yin 47
thunderbolt, symbolism of 40
titles, of poems 110–11
Tripitaka 104
trouble xi, xii
truth 107, 110, 111
Tun Huang caves 8–9, 24
Tung Wah Group 104

vase (pot), symbolism of 37, 45
vegetarianism 41
virtue, assertion of 109
Virtue King Kannon 45
vision, in poems 109
visitors, concern about 99
visualization, poems as catalyst 111

Water Moon Kannon 45
white, symbolism of 38
The White Clad Kuan Yin 37–8
willow, symbolism of 38–9, 40, 45
The Willow Branch Kuan Yin 39
woman, place of:
    in Buddhism 18
    in Taoism 19
world-view, in poems 109
Wu Cheng'en 103–4

Zoroastrianism 23

INDEX TO POEMS

After the Gold 211
After the Grey 140
As the Spirit Moves 171
Awakening 205

Balance 176
Be Yourself (says the poet) 126
The Beacon of Truth 216
Being Who You Are 194
Beyond Class or Creed 138
Beyond Reason 144
Blessing 188
Breathe 139
Burn Out 219

The Chance of the Morning 190
The Chess Game 164
Collaboration 177

Danger Mountain 207
The Demon of Hiding 161
Discrimination 214
Divinity 163
Dryness and Understanding 142

The Face of Power 208
The Family 175
Fate 184
Five Seasons 189
Flesh is Grass 131
The Flying One 122
Food for Prayer 137
Fucking Up 204

Gold 149
The Guardians 199

The Heart of It 152
The Helper 166

Illusion 146
Immortality 143
In the Circle's Round 129
In the Clear 134

In the Darkness 125
In Passing 158
In Perfect Time 147
In Reality 197
In the Shadow 192
Inferno 180
Into the Green 135
Invisible World 148
It's You 130

The Jackpot 209

King and Queen 160
Kuan Yin's Assurance 156
Kuan Yin's Promise 173
Kuan Yin's Warning 150

A Last Word 220
The Living Image 217
Living the Tao 128
The Lovers 196
Lucky One 133

The Man Himself 182
The Middle Way 187
Morality 154

Not the Way 183

Ordinary and Extraordinary 168
Over your Head 191
An Overview 145

The Phoenix 213
Presence 153
Pricking the Bubble 174
The Prize of Life 181

Rainbow Mountain 210
Reaching the End 215
The Recluse 157
Relaxation 151
Reversed 200
The Right Place 179

Shaken 206
Simplicity 198
Speeding 186
Starting Over 124
Sweetness 165

Thawing 170
The Time Waster 172
To the Devotee 121
Together 141
Trapped 218
The Traveller 123
Turn Around 132

Undeserved 162
The Unknown Story 201
Unready 159

Visible and Invisible 203

Wakefulness 185
The Water Lily 202
Wherever You Go 127
Wisdom 169
With Love 155
With a Smile 193
Wonder 136
The Worker 212
The World Teacher 167
The Wrong Way Up 195

Your Own Authority 178